Ukraine

Ukraine

BY DEBORAH KENT

Enchantment of the World™
Second Series

CHILDREN'S PRESS®

An Imprint of Scholastic Inc.

New York   Toronto   London   Auckland   Sydney
Mexico City   New Delhi   Hong Kong
Danbury, Connecticut

Frontispiece: **Kyivan Cave Monastery**

Consultant: Volodymyr Kravchenko, Director, Canadian Institute of Ukrainian Studies, University of Alberta, Edmonton, Alberta, Canada

Please note: All statistics are as up-to-date as possible at the time of publication.

Book production by The Design Lab

Library of Congress Cataloging-in-Publication Data
Kent, Deborah.
  Ukraine / by Deborah Kent.
    pages cm. — (Enchantment of the world)
  Includes bibliographical references and index.
  Audience: Grades 4–6.
  ISBN 978-0-531-21251-6 (library binding)
 1. Ukraine—Juvenile literature. 2. Ukraine—History—Juvenile literature. 3. Ukraine—
Civilization—Juvenile literature. I. Title.
  DK508.515.K46 2015
  947.7—dc23   2014031111

1 2 3 4 5 6 7 8 9 10 R 24 23 22 21 20 19 18 17 16 15

Hutsul musician

Contents

Left to right: **Traditional dancing, forest, Lviv, Mount Hoverla, watermelon harvest**

CHAPTER 1

The Fighting Poet

WHEN I DIE, BURY ME
On a grave mound
Amid the wide-wide steppe
In my beloved Ukraine,
In a place from where the wide-tilled fields
And the Dnieper and its steep banks
Can be seen and
Its roaring rapids heard.

These lines were written by the beloved Ukrainian poet Taras Shevchenko (1814–1861). Shevchenko grew up in dire poverty. He and his family lived as serfs, or virtual slaves, on the huge estate of a wealthy landowner. Sometimes the master of the estate ordered young Taras to be tied up and beaten with a stick. Through his years of bondage, Shevchenko's thoughts and ambitions remained free. By studying in secret, he learned to read and write. He also painted pictures and rendered watercolors on canvas.

The region of Ukraine where Shevchenko lived was then part of the vast Russian Empire. At the same time, much of what is now western Ukraine was under the rule of the Habsburg Empire, based in Austria. In his poems, Shevchenko urged his countrymen to seek freedom and independence. He was arrested and imprisoned because of his writings, which endeared him all the more to the Ukrainian people.

On the Edge of Europe

Ukraine lies in eastern Europe, on the northern shore of the Black Sea. Throughout most of the twentieth century, Ukraine was part of the Union of Soviet Socialist Republics (USSR), also known as the Soviet Union, a large country that stretched all the way across Asia and into Europe. The Soviet

Western Ukraine is the most mountainous region in the country.

Union dissolved in 1991, and in its place are fifteen different nations. The largest of these, and the one that dominated during the Soviet era, is Russia.

In the years after becoming independent, Ukraine became more closely aligned with Europe. Some people in Ukraine, however, felt a greater connection to Russia. In 2014, pro-Russian forces became dominant in Crimea, a peninsula that juts from southern Ukraine into the Black Sea. In March, the Crimean parliament voted to secede from Ukraine and join the Russian Federation. Russia quickly annexed Crimea, despite protests from governments around the world.

Protesters in Kharkiv, in eastern Ukraine, carry Ukrainian flags to show support for their nation. Many people in the city, however, feel more closely connected to Russia.

Trouble and Triumph

The annexation of Crimea is just the most recent act in Ukraine's long and troubled history. Over the centuries, it has been invaded, divided, and absorbed by one neighboring nation after another. Sometimes it has disappeared from the political map entirely. Yet Ukraine has always lived on in the hearts of its people. On March 9, 2014, thousands of Ukrainians gathered in towns and cities to celebrate Taras Shevchenko's two hundredth birthday. "As well as [Shevchenko] being such a great writer, he was a great patriot," one young woman said. The Russians "could not stifle his love for Ukraine."

Ukrainians enjoy music, the arts, and good food. They cherish the stories of the heroic men and women who have kept the nation's spirit alive. The story of Ukraine is one of heartbreak and courage, tragedy and triumph.

In recent years, parts of eastern Ukraine have seen frequent fighting between separatists and Ukrainian forces. In western cities such as Lviv, however, life goes on as usual.

CHAPTER 2

On the Steppe

FOR THE MOST PART, UKRAINE IS A FLAT COUNTRY. Only about 5 percent of its land is mountainous. Ukraine's level terrain and its geographical location have contributed to its history of turmoil. Ukraine serves as a gateway between Asia to the east and Europe to the west. Over the centuries one plundering army after another has marched over the Ukrainian plains, or steppe.

Geography has even influenced the nation's name. According to many historians, the word *Ukraine* is derived from a term in the Old East Slavic language meaning "borderlands."

The Lay of the Land

Sprawling over 233,090 square miles (603,700 square kilometers) including the Crimean Peninsula, Ukraine is about the size of the U.S. state of Texas. It is the largest country completely within Europe. To the south of Ukraine spread

Opposite: **Much of the Ukrainian steppe is now farmland.**

What's in a Word?

A vast grassland called the Eurasian Steppe covers much of eastern Europe. The steppe stretches all the way from Hungary in the west to China in the east and spreads across most of Ukraine. The steppe has a semiarid climate, meaning it receives 10 to 20 inches (25 to 50 centimeters) of rain each year. This relatively low rainfall supports short grasses and small trees. Tall grasses and dense forests are not able to grow there.

Bukovel, in southwestern Ukraine, is the nation's largest ski resort. More than a million people ski there every year.

the Black Sea and the Sea of Azov. Ukraine shares a long border with Russia to the east and northeast. It is bordered by Belarus to the northwest; Poland, Slovakia, and Hungary to the west; and Romania and Moldova to the southwest.

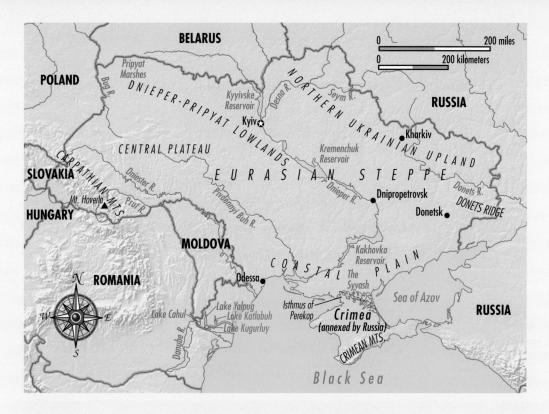

Ukraine's Geographic Features

Area: 233,090 square miles (603,700 sq km), including Crimea

Greatest Distance North to South: 550 miles (885 km)

Greatest Distance East to West: 830 miles (1,335 km)

Length of Coastline: 1,800 miles (2,900 km)

Highest Elevation: Mount Hoverla, 6,762 feet (2,061 m) above sea level

Lowest Elevation: Sea level along the Black Sea

Longest River: Dnieper, about 680 miles (1,095 km) within Ukraine

Largest Lake: Yalpug, 58 square miles (150 sq km)

Highest Recorded Temperature: 108°F (42°C) at Luhansk on August 12, 2010

Lowest Recorded Temperature: −26°F (−32°C) in Kyiv, February 9, 1929

From North to South

Geographers divide Ukraine's land into six major regions: the Dnieper-Pripyat Lowlands, the Northern Ukrainian Upland, the Central Plateau, the Central Carpathian Mountains, the Coastal Plain, and the Crimean Mountains.

The Dnieper-Pripyat Lowlands lie in the north. This marshy region serves as a basin for the Dnieper River, called the Dnipro in Ukrainian. It includes the Pripyat Marshes, one of the largest wetlands in Europe, much of which is in Belarus to the north. Ukraine's capital, Kyiv (also spelled Kiev), stands in the center of the lowlands.

The Northern Ukrainian Upland is a plateau, or an elevated level region between mountain ranges. It spreads over the northeast part of Ukraine and includes the border with Russia.

The Central Plateau contains some of Ukraine's best farmland. Fertile black soil called chernozem covers much of

Wetlands spread across the land in north-central Ukraine.

this region. Chernozem is a rare type of soil that contains a high proportion of humus, a rich material made from decaying grasses. The humus and mineral content in chernozem make this soil excellent for producing crops. Ukraine has about one-quarter of the world's chernozem supply. Its chernozem belt is widest in the southwest, near the border with Moldova, and narrows in the east, near Russia.

Until the nineteenth century, Ukrainians found it difficult to farm in the chernozem belt. Wooden plows could not break through the densely tangled roots of its grasses. Everything changed when steel plows came to the region. The new, strong plows enabled farmers to dig up the native grasses, slicing through the matted roots. Soon farmers were raising abundant wheat and other crops. Ukraine earned the nickname the Breadbasket of Europe because of its bountiful harvests.

The Central Carpathians are part of a long mountain chain in central and eastern Europe that arc from the Czech Republic

Ukraine's rich soil has helped make it one of the world's leading producers of wheat.

Chernozem and Organic Farming

Ukraine's chernozem is so fertile that it can grow most crops without the aid of fertilizer. Fruits and vegetables from many Ukrainian farms command high prices in European markets because they have been grown organically, without the use of artificial chemicals. Because chernozem is so valuable, some farmers have begun to sell truckloads of their soil. The soil is carted off for sale in Poland, Russia, and other countries. The sale of chernozem is illegal, but it persists.

in the west to Romania in the east. About 11 percent of the Carpathian range stands within Ukraine, in the western part of the country. Mount Hoverla, Ukraine's highest peak at 6,762 feet (2,061 meters), is part of the Carpathian chain.

The Coastal Plain is a lowland that stretches from the Black Sea to the Sea of Azov. Little rain falls on the Coastal Plain, and farms in the region require irrigation.

Climbing Hoverla

Experienced mountaineers consider Mount Hoverla, Ukraine's highest point, to be a relatively easy climb. Once a climber reaches the summit, however, he or she will encounter some of the worst weather in the country. The peak of Mount Hoverla is swept by high winds and is subject to frequent blizzards and thunderstorms. Nevertheless, each year on August 24 thousands of Ukrainians climb Mount Hoverla to celebrate their nation's independence. They stand at the highest point in the land and gaze at the view below them.

In a quick glance at a map, Crimea could be mistaken for an island. Crimea is actually a peninsula, connected to the mainland by a narrow strip of land called the Isthmus of Perekop. The Crimean Mountains rise on the southern tip of Crimea. The region is known for its spectacular cliffs. In 2014, Russia annexed Crimea, and the area remains under dispute.

Rivers and Lakes

Ukraine's most important river is the Dnieper. It flows out of Belarus in the north and all the way across Ukraine, emptying into the Black Sea in the south. The Dnieper is Europe's fourth-

In Crimea, rocky hills drop steeply into the Black Sea.

longest river, running about 1,370 miles (2,200 kilometers). Only the Volga, Danube, and Ural Rivers are longer. Within Ukraine, the Dnieper flows for about 680 miles (1,095 km), the longest of any river in Ukraine. Many cities have been built upon its banks, including Kyiv, Zaporizhzhya, and Dnipropetrovsk. The mighty Dnieper is a much-loved feature of the Ukrainian landscape and is mentioned in Ukraine's national anthem.

About three thousand lakes lie within the borders of Ukraine. The largest are Yalpug, Cahul, Kugurluy, and Katlabuh. Most lakes in Ukraine are small and shallow, and the waters tend to be muddy. Yet Ukrainians who love the outdoors often have a favorite fishing lake whose location they keep a secret.

Ice on the Dnieper River in Kyiv. The river is usually frozen in Kyiv about three months a year.

A Quick Tour of Ukraine's Cities

Kyiv, Ukraine's capital, is also its largest city, with about 2.8 million people. With 1.4 million people, Kharkiv (right) is Ukraine's second-largest city. It is located in northeastern Ukraine, near the border with Russia. Kharkiv is an industrial center where factories produce tanks and other military vehicles. It is also a leader in education and is home to many universities and museums. The city's central plaza, known as Freedom Square, is a noted landmark.

Odessa, Dnipropetrovsk, and Donetsk each have about 1 million residents. Odessa (left) is a major port on the Black Sea. For centuries, Odessa shipped Ukraine's farm products to cities in other parts of Europe. In modern times, Odessa attracts tourists to its beaches and lively waterfront. The city's most famous landmark is the Potemkin Stairs, a magnificent stone staircase leading down to the harbor.

Dnipropetrovsk lies on the Dnieper, in central Ukraine. Until the 1990s, Dnipropetrovsk was largely closed to visitors. It was the site of extensive nuclear and missile research for the Soviet Union, and Soviet leaders wanted to keep this work secret. Today, the atmosphere is much more open. Families and visitors enjoy the large Taras Shevchenko Park. The city is today a major industrial center, producing iron, vehicles, agricultural equipment, and much more.

Donetsk, in eastern Ukraine, is a coal and steel center. The city is known for its gardens and is nicknamed the City of a Million Roses.

Ukrainians remove snow from a sidewalk in Kyiv. Snow falls in Kyiv an average of seventy-three days a year.

Rain, Snow, and Sunshine

Occasionally a serious drought strikes Ukraine, disturbing its reputation as a breadbasket. However, long rainless periods are relatively rare. Normally rainfall is heaviest during June and July. Precipitation (the total accumulation of rain and snowfall) ranges from 30 inches (76 cm) in the north to 9 inches (23 cm) in the south.

In general, Ukraine has warm summers and cold, sometimes snowy winters. In eastern Ukraine, the temperature reaches an average daily high of about 28 degrees Fahrenheit (–2 degrees Celsius) in January and 80°F (27°C) in July. In the west, the climate is a bit milder. The southern shore of Crimea is the warmest region in Ukraine. It almost never snows in the south, and the beaches draw visitors from around the country.

Environmental Troubles

Pollution is a major concern in Ukraine. Rivers are also polluted as poorly treated sewage pours into them or fertilizer washes into them from farm fields. Coal-burning factories and other industries, particularly in the eastern part of the country, send pollutants into the air. Much of the machinery they use is old, and the companies say it would be too expensive to replace it with modern technology that is less harmful. Likewise, many of the cars on the road are old and release far more pollutants than modern cars do. The air pollution is so bad that people in eastern cities such as Mariupol and Donetsk sometimes complain of the stench in the air. Despite their complaints, however, few environmental controls have been put into place.

Smoke pours from chimneys at a factory in eastern Ukraine.

CHAPTER 3

Beasts, Birds, Fishes, and Forests

U KRAINE IS HOME TO A RICH VARIETY OF PLANT
and animal species, and Ukrainians value their nation's forests and wildlife. The Ukrainian constitution declares that the government has a responsibility to ensure the safety of the environment. Furthermore, it calls upon all Ukrainian citizens to cause no harm to nature. Despite these good intentions, however, the plants and animals of Ukraine face many threats from the human population.

Diversity of Species

Scientists estimate that about thirty thousand plant species and forty-five thousand animal species live in Ukraine. Where these species live depends upon many factors, including climate and altitude. The shores of the Black Sea and the Sea of Azov are rich areas for biodiversity, or the variety of species. The Carpathian Mountains region is another part of the country where many kinds of plants and animals flourish.

Opposite: **A foggy forest in the Carpathian Mountains. Spruce, pine, and beech are common trees in Ukrainian forests.**

Biosphere Reserves

The biosphere is the part of the earth that can support living things. It reaches from the depths of the ocean to most of the earth's mountain peaks. The United Nations Educational, Scientific and Cultural Organization (UNESCO) has established biosphere reserves throughout the world to protect environments where nature and people can live in harmony.

Since 1984, UNESCO has created five biosphere reserves in Ukraine. These include Askania-Nova (right), a reserve that protects a pristine section of the steppe, and the Carpathian Biosphere Reserve, a mountainous area rich in plant and mushroom life. Three more biosphere reserves span the borders between Ukraine and neighboring countries. For example, West Polesie Biosphere Reserve protects a region filled with lakes and bogs in the area where Ukraine, Poland, and Belarus meet.

Forests and Grasslands

The most heavily forested region of Ukraine is in the Carpathian Mountains of the west. Pine, oak, and birch trees grow there. Mountain meadows lie in the higher reaches of these mountains.

The north and northwest is a mix of woodlands and open land. Many kinds of trees grow there, including oak, elm, maple, birch, and beech.

On the steppe grow scattered clusters of oak, pine, and hornbeam. But mostly, this region is covered with grasses such as fescue and feather grass. In the spring, the steppe is ablaze with anemones, cornflowers, wild hollyhocks, and Madonna lilies.

Ironwood

The hornbeam is a deciduous tree (a tree that sheds its leaves in the fall) that is related to the birch. Most hornbeam species grow in Asia and eastern Europe. Because the wood of the hornbeam is very hard, it is sometimes known as ironwood. It is used to make cutting boards, tool handles, coach wheels, parquet flooring, and chess pieces.

The Animal World

About forty-five thousand different animal species have been identified in Ukraine. The vast majority of these are small creatures such as insects, spiders, worms, and snails. Fish such as perch, pike, and carp fill the lakes. Ukraine also has many kinds of snakes, lizards, and birds. Hawks and eagles sail above

Nature's Remedies

Long ago, some people in Ukraine discovered that certain wild plants had the power to cure diseases. In the 1930s and 1940s Ukraine faced a shortage of medicines. Scientists began to study the healing plants that people had relied on for centuries. They discovered about 250 plants in Ukraine with medicinal properties. Many of these plants are now used in the manufacture of drugs. Wild poppy (left), belladonna, and jimsonweed are used to make painkillers. Shrub aloe, juniper, and wormwood are helpful in treating some skin disorders. Viburnum, yarrow, and nettle are used in drugs that stop bleeding. St. John's wort helps fight a wide variety of illnesses, including liver disease and depression.

Four European bee-eaters perch on a branch in Ukraine. The birds catch bees, wasps, and other insects in midair and then return to a branch to remove the stingers before eating the insects.

the steppe, and pelicans, gulls, and cormorants nest along the shores of the Black Sea and the Sea of Azov. Grouse, partridges, geese, and owls are also common.

Over one hundred species of mammals are native to Ukraine. They range from the tiny gray dwarf hamster to the huge wisent, or European bison. Deer graze on the steppe

Second Chance for a Giant

The wisent, or European bison, is a magnificent animal with long, curving horns. It can measure nearly 10 feet (3 m) in length and stand 5 to 7 feet high (1.5 to 2 m) at the shoulder. The wisent disappeared from Ukraine by the end of the nineteenth century, and by the 1920s no wild wisents survived anywhere in Europe. However, a few wisents still lived in zoos. After years of breeding, small herds have been reestablished in many parts of their former range. Today, about 250 wisents live in Ukraine.

and in the forests. Carnivorous, or meat-eating, animals in Ukraine include the weasel-like stoat, the red fox, the wildcat, and the gray wolf. They feed on a variety of creatures, including the many rodents that make their home in Ukraine, such as gophers, mice, and jerboas.

The stoat preys on creatures such as rabbits, voles, and pikas.

CHAPTER 4

Strife and Hope

LONG BEFORE WRITTEN RECORDS, THE LAND NOW known as Ukraine served as a gateway between east and west. Roving bands of hunters passed through the region as early as 160,000 years ago. Many of these hunters were migrating from Asia into Europe.

As humans developed agriculture, the steppe of Ukraine lured farmers and herders. The Trypillian culture arose in Ukraine some six thousand years ago. The Trypillian people grew wheat, oats, and other grains, as well as beans, peas, and apricots.

Many Migrations

Men and women from distant regions came to what is now Ukraine. The Cimmerians moved onto the southern Ukrainian steppe from Asia, perhaps as early as the tenth century BCE. They were driven out by the Scythians, from central Asia, who controlled the steppe between the seventh and third centuries BCE. In the third century BCE, the

Opposite: **Trypillian culture is renowned for its red and orange pottery, often decorated with curving lines.**

Scythians were conquered by another central Asian group, the Sarmatians. Greek colonies were founded along the Black Sea beginning in the seventh century BCE. Some of these cities, such as Tyras and Olbia, became thriving trading centers.

Other groups came in the following centuries. Goths came from the north and Huns from the east. Slavs began arriving from the west beginning in the sixth century CE. They practiced agriculture and built settlements, including what became Kyiv.

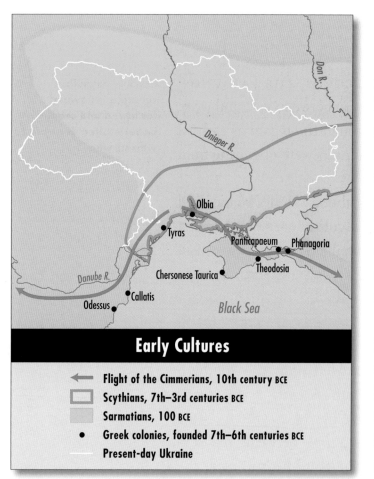

Early Cultures

⬅ Flight of the Cimmerians, 10th century BCE
▢ Scythians, 7th–3rd centuries BCE
▨ Sarmatians, 100 BCE
● Greek colonies, founded 7th–6th centuries BCE
— Present-day Ukraine

Kyivan Rus

In the ninth century, Varangians from Scandinavia, in northern Europe, came to dominate the area around Kyiv. They controlled international trade through the region and were central in forming the region's first state, called Kyivan Rus, in the mid-ninth century. Kyivan Rus gradually expanded, spreading north all the way to the Baltic Sea.

Many of the people in Kyivan Rus were pagans, who worshipped many different gods, but Christianity was spreading in the region. In 988 a Rus leader named Vladimir I, known to Ukrainians as Volodymyr the

Great, became a Christian. Kyivan Rus became part of Byzantine Christianity, which later became called Orthodox Christianity. As the Rus leaders adopted Byzantine religion, they were also influenced by Byzantine culture. New styles of art and architecture spread.

Culture flourished under the leadership of Vladimir's son, Yaroslav I, who ruled from 1036 to 1054. During this time, a code of laws was written, a library was established, and education expanded. Kyiv became a magnificent city, with buildings such as Saint Sophia Cathedral. In the eleventh century, a French bishop visiting Kyivan Rus reported, "This land is more unified, happier, stronger, and more civilized than France herself."

But the glory of Kyivan Rus did not protect it from strife. Princes fought over who should rule, until the once mighty land splintered into a dozen warring states. Weakened by

Yaroslav the Wise (seated) promoted Christianity during his reign, founding several churches and monasteries.

Strife and Hope **35**

Kyivan Rus

Kyivan Rus, 1100
Present-day Ukraine

internal conflicts, Kyivan Rus was powerless to withstand a foreign invasion. In 1240 the Tatars, a people from Asia, destroyed Kyiv and conquered the surrounding territory. The Tatars did not stay long, but they left Kyiv and the surrounding countryside in ruins.

Lithuanian and Polish Rule

In the 1300s, much of northern and central Ukraine fell under the control of the grand duchy of Lithuania, a growing power to the north. Lithuania also took over the land that is now Belarus. Together, the Ukrainians and Belarusians were known as Ruthenians. Lithuania did not have tight control over Ruthenian lands, and, in fact, elite members of Ruthenian society were part of the ruling class. Meanwhile, Lithuanian and Ruthenian cultures were melding, and many pagan Lithuanians were converting to Orthodox Christianity.

Meanwhile, another power, Poland, controlled Galicia, a region in what is now western Ukraine. Unlike the Lithuanians, the Poles were Roman Catholic. Gradually, interaction increased between the Polish and Lithuanian states, leading to the spread of Catholicism among the Lithuanians. By 1413, Orthodox Christians were no longer allowed in the highest levels of government, diminishing the power of the Ruthenians. In 1569, the two states finally merged into the Polish-Lithuanian Commonwealth, which was dominated by Polish culture. Most Ukrainian lands were now under Polish rule. As Polish culture spread, many upper-class Ruthenians became Catholic. The peasants remained Orthodox.

Polish leaders established a system of serfdom that bound Ukrainian farmers to work the land on Polish-owned estates. The serfs had to give most of their crops to the landowners, and they could not move or change occupations without permission.

Rebellion

To resist their Polish overlords, some serfs fled to the eastern steppe, where they joined a group of men known as Cossacks. The Cossacks hunted, fished, and countered Tatar raids from the east. They also supported the Orthodox Church. In 1648, a Cossack named Bohdan Khmelnytsky led Cossacks and peasants in a revolt against their

Polish-Lithuanian Commonwealth

▨ Polish-Lithuanian Commonwealth, 1619
— Present-day Ukraine

Polish rulers. Khmelnytsky's forces made their way across Ukraine, and in 1649 entered Kyiv.

Khmelnytsky wanted to become independent from Poland, but as the battles wore on, his forces grew tired. He needed allies. In 1654, he signed an agreement with Russia. Under this agreement, Ukraine would come under the protection of the Russian tsar, or emperor, but would remain self-governing. But still strife continued.

Division

Ukraine broke with Russia in 1658, but chaos only grew. The late 1600s were so bad that Ukrainians call it the Ruin. In 1667, Ukraine was partitioned. The region to the west of the

Bohdan Khmelnytsky led a rebellion against Poland and hoped to create an independent Cossack state.

As a young man, Ivan Mazepa served in the court of the Polish king. In his twenties, he returned to Ukraine to work for a Cossack hetman before becoming a hetman himself.

Dnieper River came under Polish rule. Russia took possession of the region east of the Dnieper, along with Kyiv.

The Russian side of Ukraine still had some autonomy. The Cossacks elected a leader, called a hetman. Ivan Mazepa was elected hetman in 1687. During his reign, art, literature, and education flourished. As Mazepa became more powerful, he hoped to reunite the two parts of Ukraine. This was not to be, however. The Russian tsar Peter I was centralizing his own power, which threatened Ukrainian autonomy. Mazepa sided with Sweden in a war against Russia. When Russia was triumphant, Mazepa was forced to flee.

At various times in history, Cossacks both engaged in peasant revolts and served in the military of the Russian Empire.

Russian Rule

In the years after, the hetmans became weaker, and the Russian Empire began governing eastern Ukraine more directly. Russia gained even greater control in the late 1700s when Poland lost all of its Ukrainian lands. At this time, Russia gained control of most of western Ukraine, while Galicia fell under the rule of Austria's Habsburg Empire.

Most of Ukraine was now part of the Russian Empire, its territories governed as Russian provinces. Many members of the Ukrainian ruling elite joined the high government ranks of Russia. Meanwhile, peasants continued to suffer. There were sometimes uprisings, and finally, in 1861, the peasants were freed from serfdom. They now had full rights, but many were burdened with debt and could not buy land of their own to farm.

Ukraine's Jewish population was also suffering. It endured widespread poverty and discrimination. Jews were limited in where they could live and what jobs they could have.

There were also periodic waves of anti-Jewish violence called pogroms. Because of the poverty and violence, many Jewish people left Ukraine.

In the nineteenth century, Ukrainian culture began blossoming. The work of writers such as Taras Shevchenko helped spur the growth of Ukrainian nationalism. In response, Russian leaders launched a program called Russification. As part of this program, the Russian authorities tried to ban the Ukrainian language in many settings. All instruction in Ukrainian schools was done in Russian. By the late 1800s, Ukrainian-language books, newspapers, and performances were not allowed.

The first pogrom took place in 1881. In Kyiv, rioters destroyed the homes and businesses of many Jews.

The Gathering Storm

In the late 1800s, most of Europe enjoyed great progress. Schools opened, and even the children of peasant families learned to read. Railroads crisscrossed the land, and factories sprouted in cities. But Ukraine and most of the Russian Empire lagged behind much of the continent. Schools were few, and a handful of wealthy landowners ruled over millions of landless peasants. The grinding injustice fueled an all-consuming rage. Russia was ripe for an uprising.

Like a raging storm, an uprising shook the Russian Empire in 1905. In the Black Sea, sailors manning the battleship *Potemkin* mutinied against their officers and seized the vessel. The rebel sailors took the ship to the port of Odessa, where

A peasant family at work in a field in eastern Ukraine in the early twentieth century

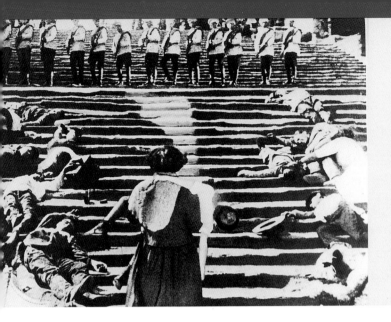

the people cheered them as liberators. Infuriated, Russian tsar Nicholas II sent troops to Odessa to quell the revolt. The rebels were executed, along with hundreds of Ukrainians who had supported them. The tsar was victorious, but the entire Russian Empire remained tense.

Revolution

In 1914, Europe was rocked by the beginning of a shattering conflict that would become known as World War I. It was a war of alliances that saw Europe split into two primary camps. Russia (including most of what is now Ukraine), Great Britain, and France fought against an alliance headed by Germany and the Austro-Hungarian Empire, which included Galicia.

Russia was poorly prepared for a major war. Its soldiers toted old, outdated weapons. Most of the troops were peasants who were angry over the cruel conditions they faced at home. Not surprisingly, the Russian armies suffered a series of crushing defeats in the field.

Meanwhile, conditions on the Russian homefront grew steadily worse. Because of the constant battles, two million homeless refugees roamed the roads. Many of the refugees were army deserters who had kept their weapons. In the countryside, fields were destroyed. Cities ran out of bread, the Russian staple food.

In March 1917, long lines of men and women waited for bread rations in the city of Petrograd (today's St. Petersburg). The people standing in line knew that the bakeries had bread, but the rich and privileged were being served first. When the people lost patience, riots broke out. Officers ordered troops to fire into the crowd. At least eighty people were killed.

The rioting continued, but during the next few days, fewer and fewer soldiers were willing to fight the rioters. Rather than firing on them as they had been ordered, some soldiers joined the rioters and fought against the authorities. A revolution shook the Russian Empire.

Spearhead of a Movement

In the background of the Russian Revolution loomed one man, Vladimir Lenin (1870–1924). Lenin had been born into a well-established family in Russia. As a young man, he studied the works of the German philosopher Karl Marx. Marx advocated Communism, a system in which workers collectively owned their factories and farmers collectively owned their fields. Lenin became a dedicated Communist.

Soviet Union, 1989

Soviet Socialist Republic (SSR) — Present-day borders

Kaliningrad (RSFSR)
Lithuanian SSR
Estonian SSR
Latvian SSR
Moldavian SSR
Belorussian SSR
Ukrainian SSR
Georgian SSR
Armenian SSR
Azerbaijan SSR
Turkmen SSR
Uzbek SSR
Kazakh SSR
Kirghiz SSR
Tajik SSR
Russian Soviet Federative Socialist Republic (RSFSR)

Arctic Ocean
& Bering Sea
Sea of Okhotsk
Sea of Japan
Black Sea
Caspian Sea

A Taste of Independence

A new provisional government took power in Russia. It allowed greater freedom than the tsarist government had. With their newfound freedom, Ukrainians formed political, professional, and cultural organizations. Representatives of these organizations formed the Central Rada, or council. Two weeks after Communists seized power in Russia in November 1917, the Central Rada declared that Ukraine was now the Ukrainian National Republic. In January 1918, the Ukrainian National Republic declared complete independence.

The situation in Russia soon turned into a civil war. The tsar and his family were executed, the war raged on, and the Communists eventually emerged victorious.

The Ukrainian National Republic did not survive this. Russian armies seized eastern and central Ukraine in 1920.

In 1922, the Communists established the Union of Soviet Socialist Republics (USSR), which included most of Ukraine.

In the USSR

During the 1920s, Soviet leaders wanted to gain favor with the non-Russians in the USSR. To do this, Soviet authorities encouraged the use of native languages. After a long period of suppression, Ukrainian was suddenly the official language in Ukraine's schools and places of business.

Ukrainians were thrilled that their language was permitted in public places once again. Yet the sudden transition was not a smooth one. A student in Kharkiv remembered, "Even those who, like myself, had spoken Ukrainian from childhood, were not accustomed to its use as a medium of study. Our local tongue simply had not caught up with modern knowledge; its vocabulary was unsuited to the purposes of electrotechnics, chemistry, aerodynamics, physics, and most other sciences."

Nonetheless, the change made a profound difference. For the first time, many Ukrainians learned to read and write in their native language. Ukrainian literature blossomed.

The Great Famine

In 1928, Soviet leader Joseph Stalin launched his first five-year plan for agricultural and industrial development. One such plan after another would follow. Stalin's program called for rapid industrialization, the collectivization of farms, and the redistribution of farm products throughout the country. In practice, the plan meant that Ukraine's small farms, which had

Ukrainian workers harvest crops on a collectivized farm, while officials keep track of the work.

been owned and worked by families for generations, would be merged and tended by large groups of farmers. "People didn't want to enter these collective farms at all," recalled Hanna Hrytsay, who was seven years old when collectivization began in 1929. She continued, "They were forced to. [The soldiers] took everything—land, grain, plows, animals. And as if that weren't enough they took the bread out of the house."

Many independent farmers of Ukraine rebelled against this collective farming program. The Soviet authorities punished the rebellious farmers without mercy. They burst into farmhouses and barns to confiscate grain and livestock. Many peasants who rebelled against collectivization or were considered "wealthy" because they had a stable or several head of livestock were deported. They were sent away to desolate places such as Siberia, in northern Russia. By the mid-1930s, about one hundred thousand Ukrainian families had been deported.

Soviet authorities demanded that Ukrainian farmers produce more grain than was possible. When the Ukrainians failed to meet the grain quotas, their houses were searched and their grain stocks were confiscated. Hungry Ukrainians were left with no food to feed themselves. Furthermore, crops harvested in Ukraine were not available to feed hungry Ukrainians. Instead, the grain crops were shipped elsewhere.

This bitter chapter in Ukrainian history is called the Great Famine. In 1932 and 1933, an estimated four to five million Ukrainians starved to death as Soviet officials hauled away their

A row of carts carry away bread that has been confiscated from Ukrainian peasants in 1932.

food supplies. Miron Dolot, a Ukrainian who lived through the famine as a boy, wrote, "One could see strange funeral processions: children pulling homemade hand-wagons with the bodies of their dead parents in them, or the parents carting the bodies of their children. There were no coffins; no burial ceremonies performed by priests. The bodies of the starved were just deposited in a large common grave, one upon the other."

In spite of earlier gestures toward encouraging the Ukrainian language, many Soviet leaders harbored a deep distrust of Ukraine and its culture. Ukrainians were not Russians, and many of them did not embrace Communism. The Great Famine may have been Stalin's way of weakening Ukraine and stifling any hope of resistance.

Millions of Ukrainians died during the Great Famine. This event is often called the Holodomor, which means "to kill by starvation."

Soviet troops attack
German forces in a
Ukrainian village in 1942.

Another War

In September 1939, Germany invaded Poland, marking the onset of World War II. The Germans overran Galicia, which was then part of Poland.

Germany was commanded by the Nazi dictator Adolf Hitler. At first Stalin joined Hitler in his war against Poland. The Polish armies were quickly defeated. Germany and the USSR divided Poland between them, but Hitler was not satisfied. His true goal was to expand his country east to the USSR and to seize the fertile farmlands of Ukraine.

In 1941, German armies swept into the Soviet Union. When the Germans entered Ukraine, some Ukrainians greeted them as liberators. Villagers showered the German soldiers with flowers and sang songs of celebration. The Ukrainians hated Stalin and the Communists. The memory of the Great Famine was fresh in their minds. Any enemy of the Soviets, they assumed, must be a friend of Ukraine.

But the warm welcome soon became outrage. The Germans captured thousands of Ukrainian peasants, crowded them into cattle cars, and shipped them to labor camps in Germany. Farmers from Germany moved onto Ukraine's newly vacant land.

After this appalling treatment, most Ukrainians returned to the Soviet fold. Many Ukrainians fought in the Soviet army. Others joined secret underground units and fought the Germans by attacking their supply lines. Some Ukrainians refused to fight for either the Germans or the Soviets. Tens of thousands of Ukrainians joined the Ukrainian Insurgent Army and fought the enemies on both fronts.

World War II ended in 1945. It had ravaged Ukraine. Some eighteen thousand villages were destroyed, and 6.8 million Ukrainians lost their lives to fighting, hunger, and disease.

The Fate of Ukraine's Jews

While Germany's leader Adolf Hitler was busy waging war against other nations in Europe, he also launched a vicious campaign to destroy the Jews of Europe. Jewish people in Germany, Poland, France, and the Netherlands were arrested and transported to concentration camps. Some were forced to perform heavy labor, while others were murdered outright. In Ukraine, Germany's occupying army singled out Jews for slaughter. Almost one million Ukrainian Jews were executed, usually by machine gun fire. In the largest single massacre, September 29 to 30, 1941, at Babi Yar ravine in Kyiv, more than thirty-three thousand Jews were killed. Each year, Ukraine holds a ceremony marking the massacre (left).

After the War

The end of the war in Europe ushered in a new period of world tension called the Cold War. This was a struggle between the Communist Soviet Union and the anti-Communist United States for power and influence. The two powerful nations were pitted against each other, always on the brink of combat. Americans, Canadians, and western Europeans tended to think of their Cold War opponents simply as "the Russians." They rarely reflected that the Soviet Union was composed of separate republics, most of which had joined the USSR against their will.

Joseph Stalin died in 1953, and Nikita Khrushchev became the new premier of the Soviet Union. Khrushchev was born

Soviet forces parade through Moscow, the capital of the Soviet Union, in 1956. During the Cold War, the Soviet Union had the largest active army in the world.

near Ukraine, and he once served as governor of the republic. Under Khrushchev, more Ukrainians gained power in the Soviet government. Khrushchev promised to be more flexible and allow Soviet citizens greater freedom. In a secret speech, he denounced the repressive nature of Stalin's rule. Hundreds of thousands of Ukrainians who had been sent away to camps were allowed to return. Meanwhile, industry was growing in Ukraine, and the economy improved.

In 1964, the aging Khrushchev fell from power, and a new leader, Leonid Brezhnev, took charge. Brezhnev had been born in the Ukrainian city of Dniprodzerhynsk. He recognized Ukraine as one of the leading Soviet republics in terms of its industrial and agricultural potential. Yet he had no sympathy for Ukrainian nationalists who hoped to steer their republic away from the USSR.

Soviet leader Nikita Khrushchev (center) tours a mine in Ukraine in 1959. Khrushchev had spent many years working in Ukraine earlier in his career.

Two explosions rocked the nuclear reactor at Chernobyl. About two hundred thousand people were permanently evacuated to escape the radiation.

Tragedy at Chernobyl

By the early 1980s, Ukraine's economy, and the Soviet Union's economy as a whole, was in decline. Ukraine's problems increased in April 1986, when a fire broke out at the Chernobyl Nuclear Power Plant near Kyiv. The fire caused an explosion that ripped apart a nuclear reactor and released deadly clouds of radioactive particles into the air. Government reports claimed that thirty-one people had died from radiation sickness and that two hundred more were injured. Experts around the world suspected that the casualty figures were far higher than that. While scientists and political leaders tried to sort out the truth, winds carried the poisonous clouds over much of the western Soviet Union and into central and northern Europe.

The Chernobyl disaster was the deadliest nuclear-power accident in history. Thousands of people in Russia, Ukraine, and central Europe developed thyroid cancer as a result of exposure to radiation. Most of these cancer victims were children. The Soviet government evacuated the city of Chernobyl and created a "Zone of Exclusion" some 37 miles (60 km) across. Yet crews of firefighters, engineers, and other workers were ordered to enter the zone and work to secure the reactor in an attempt to contain the toxic radiation. Today, plants and animals in the Zone of Exclusion continue to show high levels of radioactivity.

Europe's Biggest Wildlife Sanctuary

After the nuclear disaster at Chernobyl, about three hundred thousand people were evacuated from the city and the surrounding area. They were forced to abandon their homes and possessions, to move to new communities and try to build new lives. A few people, most of them elderly, obtained permits allowing them to stay. About two years after the nuclear accident, the people who remained in the vicinity reported seeing deer, eagles, and even wolves. These wild animals had vanished from the region centuries before. Somehow they discovered that humans had gone away, and they hurried to fill the vacuum. By 2014, bears, elk, moose, and rare wildcats called lynxes had returned. Scientists found some deformities and illnesses in small animals such as mice and insects. Strangely, most of the larger animals appeared to be healthy, although their bodies had a level of radioactivity that would be considered lethal to humans. The radioactive environment seems to be less dangerous to wildlife than living close to humans and human activity.

Independence at Last

In 1985, Mikhail Gorbachev became the leader of the Soviet Union. As the nation's leader, Gorbachev launched a policy of *glasnost*, or openness, which gave the people of the USSR more freedom of choice. With this freedom came a rise in nationalism among the various Soviet republics, and the USSR began to collapse. The Baltic republic of Latvia was one of the first to challenge Soviet authority. In December 1986, young Latvians took to the streets, chanting "Soviet Russia out! Free Latvia!" Just a few years earlier, such a dem-

Mikhail Gorbachev speaks to a crowd in Lviv in 1989, promoting his reform policies.

A Ukrainian holds a splattered picture of Vladimir Lenin at a demonstration in 1991 in Kyiv celebrating Ukraine's declaration of independence.

onstration would have been broken up by troops and tanks. Now the unrest spread to other Soviet republics. The Soviet Union, which had lasted seventy years, was being torn apart from within.

While much of the former Soviet Union was in turmoil, the people of Ukraine proceeded with their own independence movement. Ukraine's break with Soviet rule was largely a peaceful transition. On August 24, 1991, the Ukrainian parliament declared Ukraine independent. In December, voters were given ballots that posed the question, "Do you support the act of Declaration of Independence of Ukraine?" More than 90 percent of the voters answered "Yes." Ukraine became an independent state.

Women lead a goat to market in the city of Luhansk, in eastern Ukraine, in 1996. Ukraine's economy shrank by 60 percent in the 1990s.

Turmoil

It was one thing to sever the ties with the Soviet Union. It was quite another to build a healthy new nation. Newly independent Ukraine faced a host of problems. State-supported industries that had been fostered under Soviet rule were inefficient and run by corrupt managers. Roads and bridges were in disrepair. Nothing seemed to get done unless bribes and more bribes were paid. Gradually, however, the economy stabilized.

Still Ukraine struggled. The country suffered from political corruption and a lack of political stability. In 2004, two men competed for the presidency: Viktor Yanukovych, who was closely aligned with Russia, and Viktor Yushchenko, who supported closer ties with Europe. Yanukovych was declared the winner of a runoff election, but Yushchenko's supporters claimed that the election had been rigged. They took to the streets in huge protests. The protesters wore orange, the color of Yushchenko's campaign, so the movement became known as the Orange Revolution. The Supreme Court ordered a new election, which Yushchenko won, becoming president. Yulia Tymoshenko, who had also supported the Orange Revolution, became prime minister. These three politicians would continue to vie for power in the coming years.

Protesters blocked access to a government building during the Orange Revolution of 2004.

Yanukovych became president in 2010. In November 2013, he was preparing to sign an agreement that would have given Ukraine closer ties to the European Union. But under pressure from Russia, he chose not to sign the agreement. Many Ukrainians took to the streets in protest, filling Maidan (Independence) Square in Kyiv. In the coming days and weeks, what became known as the Maidan protest movement

Protesters filled Maidan Square in Kyiv in 2013 after the Ukrainian government rejected a pact creating closer ties with the European Union.

Yulia Tymoshenko

Yulia Tymoshenko has been called Ukraine's most popular politician. She was a prominent leader in the Orange Revolution, and she later served as Ukraine's prime minister in 2005 and again from 2007 to 2010. Tymoshenko worked for Ukraine's inclusion in the European Union, which would lead it away from Russia and toward western Europe.

She ran for president against Viktor Yanukovych in 2010, but lost. In 2011, the Yanukovych government charged her with embezzlement of government funds and sentenced her to seven years in prison. The European Union, the United States, and international organizations such as Human Rights Watch claimed that the charges had been political and called for her release. Tymoshenko was released in February 2014 during the Maidan protests. The Supreme Court concluded that she had not committed any crimes after all.

expanded to other cities. The police sometimes responded to the demonstrations violently, and dozens of protesters were killed. By February 2014, Yanukovych had lost much of his power and fled to Russia.

Crisis followed crisis in Ukraine. In March, the Crimean parliament voted to secede from Ukraine and join the Russian Federation. Russia quickly annexed Crimea, but most countries around the world claimed that this was illegal. In the months that followed, pro-Russian separatists took over government buildings in several cities in eastern Ukraine. The separatists and Ukrainian forces battled for control. Only time will tell whether Ukraine can achieve peace and stability.

CHAPTER 5

Governing a Restless Nation

EVERY YEAR ON AUGUST 24, UKRAINIANS GATHER in parks and town squares to celebrate their nation's independence. Flags fly, bands play, fireworks light up the sky, and schoolchildren sing the national anthem. Parents and grandparents think back to the years before 1991, when Ukraine was controlled by the Soviet Union. During those years they hardly dared to dream of an independent Ukraine.

Opposite: **Fireworks burst over Kyiv in celebration of Independence Day.**

According to the Constitution

Shortly after Ukraine declared its independence in 1991, a commission gathered to draft a constitution. A constitution is a set of laws that determines how a nation will be governed. Ukraine's new constitution was adopted on June 28, 1996.

The Ukrainian constitution divides the government into three branches. The executive branch, headed by the president, ensures that the laws are carried out. The legislative branch, or parliament, passes the laws. The judicial branch, or court system, interprets the laws.

The constitution guarantees many rights and freedoms to the Ukrainian people. Ukrainians are ensured freedom of speech, freedom of the press, and freedom of religion. The constitution states that members of ethnic minorities are full citizens and have the right to use the language they prefer. Under the constitution, all Ukrainian citizens over the age of eighteen have the right to vote.

A Ukrainian casts a ballot during the presidential election of 2014. Petro Poroshenko, a supporter of the Maidan protests, won the election.

Ukraine's National Government

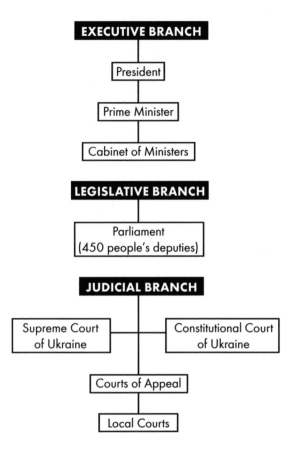

EXECUTIVE BRANCH

President

Prime Minister

Cabinet of Ministers

LEGISLATIVE BRANCH

Parliament
(450 people's deputies)

JUDICIAL BRANCH

Supreme Court of Ukraine

Constitutional Court of Ukraine

Courts of Appeal

Local Courts

Executive Branch

The president of Ukraine is chosen by popular vote for a five-year term. He or she can serve no more than two terms in a row. A presidential candidate must be at least thirty-five years old. He or she must have lived in Ukraine for ten or more years and must speak the Ukrainian language.

The president serves as commander in chief of the armed forces. The president can introduce bills into parliament and veto, or reject, bills that are passed by parliament. Parliament, however, has the power to overturn the president's veto. The

The Ukrainian Flag

The Ukrainian flag is divided evenly into two bands, one blue and one yellow. The blue upper half represents Ukraine's blue skies, and the yellow lower half signifies the nation's fields of yellow wheat. Sometimes the national flag is flown vertically on public buildings, usually along-side a local flag. When the flag is flown vertically, the blue portion is always closest to the staff.

The current flag was adopted by the Ukrainian National Republic in 1918. After the Soviet Union took over in 1922, the national flag was no longer flown. The flag became the official flag of Ukraine once again in 1992.

president also oversees the Cabinet of Ministers, and appoints its members, who are in charge of running the government. The prime minister is the head of the Cabinet of Ministers.

Ukrainian president Petro Poroshenko supports both closer ties to Europe and mending relations with Russia.

Parliament

The Verkhovna Rada, or parliament, consists of 450 members, or people's deputies. The deputies are chosen by popular election and serve five-year terms.

The Rada, as it is generally called, has a great deal of power in the Ukrainian government. Its members write laws, amend the constitution, and ratify international treaties. The Rada also elects the prime minister, who is the head of the government.

Judicial Branch

The Supreme Court of Ukraine is the highest court in the nation. The Supreme Court can review decisions made by lower courts. The court system also includes courts of appeal and local courts, where most trials are held. Ukraine also has

National Anthem

The words to Ukraine's national anthem, "The State Anthem of Ukraine," are based upon lyrics written by poet and folklorist Pavlo Chubynsky in 1862. In 1863, Mykhailo Verbytsky, a priest in the Greek Catholic Church, set Chubynsky's words to music. The Ukrainian parliament adopted the song as Ukraine's national anthem in 2003.

Ukrainian lyrics

Shche ne vmerla Ukrayiny,
ni slava, ni volya.
Shche nam, brattia ukrayintsi,
Usmikhnet'sia dolia.
Z-hynut' nashi vorozhen'ky,
Yak rosa na sontsi.
Zapanuyem i my, brattia,
U svoyiy storontsi.

Dushu y tilo my polozhym,
Za nashu svobodu.
I pokazhem, shcho my, brattia,
Kozats'koho rodu.

English translation

Ukraine's freedom has not yet perished,
Nor has her glory.
Upon us, fellow Ukrainians,
Fate shall smile once more.
Our enemies will vanish
Like dew in the sun.
And we too shall rule, brothers,
In a free land of our own.

We'll lay down our souls and bodies
To attain our freedom.
And we'll show that we, brothers,
Are of the Cossack nation.

a Constitutional Court, which interprets the constitution and ensures that laws follow its requirements.

All judges are appointed by the president to serve five-year terms, after which they are generally reappointed for life. The constitution promises Ukrainian citizens the right to a trial by jury. In practice, however, Ukraine has no jury system. Most cases are heard by one or two judges and assistants called assessors.

Judges on Ukraine's Supreme Court announce a verdict. The Supreme Court is made up of four separate groups that handle different types of cases.

Provincial and Local Government

Ukraine is divided into twenty-four oblasts, or provinces. The cities of Kyiv and Sevastopol have special status and are not part of any oblast. Crimea is an autonomous republic within Ukraine, although in 2014, it was annexed by Russia.

The constitution permits each city and village to elect its own mayor and governing council. District and regional councils support the common interests of several villages or cities. Each mayor, who is elected to a four-year term, leads an executive committee.

Vitali Klitschko was elected mayor of Kyiv in 2014. Before becoming mayor, Klitschko was a world-champion boxer.

Ukraine's Capital City

Kyiv, the capital of Ukraine, is also the largest city in the nation, with a population of about 2.8 million. The city stands on a series of wooded hills overlooking the Dnieper River.

People have been living on the site of what is now Kyiv for at least fifteen thousand years. Kyiv itself was likely founded in the sixth or seventh century CE. The city grew in importance and splendor when it was the capital of Kyivan Rus. It was destroyed during the Tatar invasion in 1240 and recovered slowly. Today, it is again thriving and is the cultural, economic, and educational heart of Ukraine.

Kyiv is a mix of old and new architecture. One of Kyiv's most beautiful buildings is the great Mariinsky Palace (bottom right), where the president holds dinners and other state functions. Next door to the palace is a building with a magnificent glass dome, the meeting place of the Verkhovna Rada. Ukrainian independence was declared in this building in 1991. The Maidan

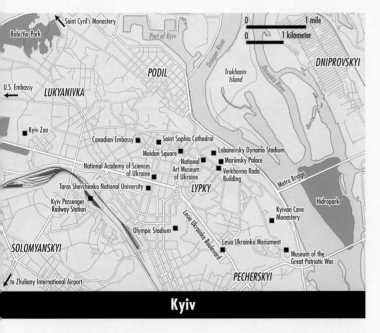
Kyiv

Nezalezhnosti, Independence Square, is the city's central gathering place (top). In 2013 and 2014 it was the scene of massive protests.

One of Kyiv's most impressive landmarks is Saint Sophia Cathedral. Construction on the cathedral began in 1037 and took approximately twenty years. The cathedral has thirteen cupolas, or small domes, which represent Jesus, who Christians believe is the son of God, and his twelve apostles, or closest followers. Another important religious site in the city is the Kyivan Cave Monastery, an Orthodox monastery founded in 1051.

Governing a Restless Nation **71**

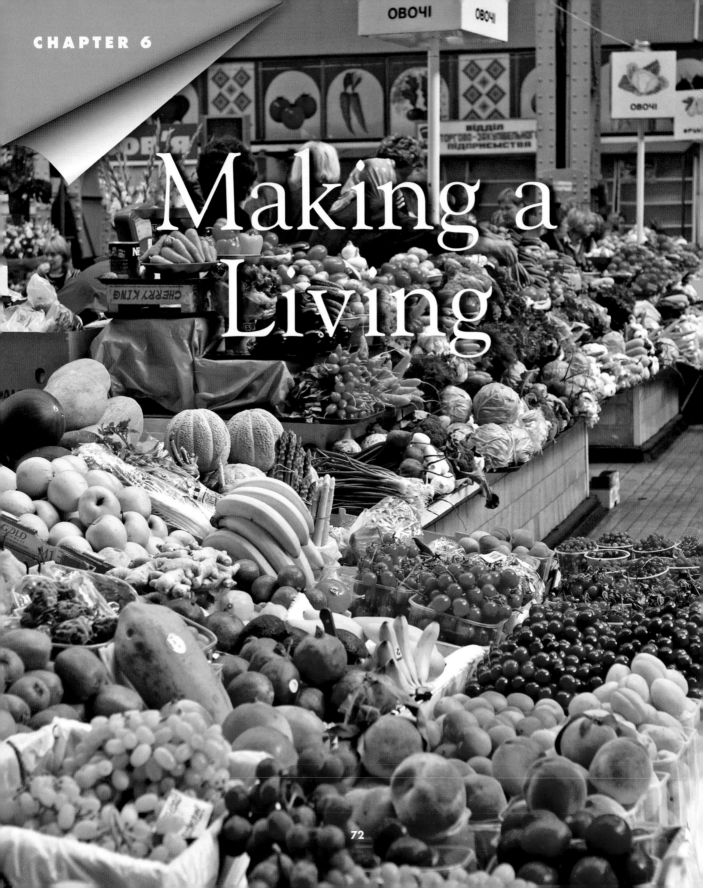

CHAPTER 6

Making a Living

U KRAINE IS BLESSED WITH SUCH RICH, FERTILE soil that it has earned the nickname the Breadbasket of Europe. It has busy factories, excellent seaports, and an extensive system of highways and railroads. Yet in the decades after independence, Ukraine's economy began to unravel. The people endured. As prices rose and incomes tumbled, Ukrainians reminded one another of an old saying, "Things will improve somehow." They determined to make the best of whatever came their way.

The Shadow Economy

When Ukraine became independent, its people were ill-prepared for a new economic reality. Under the Communist system, the state controlled most of Ukraine's agriculture, mining, and manufacturing. Instead of buying goods from official sources, many people bought goods illegally, in what is called the shadow economy.

Money Facts

Ukraine's currency is called the hryvnia (the plural is hryvni). In 2014, 1 hryvnia was worth about US$0.08, and about US$1.00 equaled about 13 hryvni.

Ukraine mints a 1-hryvnia coin, but it is seldom used. Hryvnia bills come in many denominations: 1, 5, 10, 20, 50, 100, and 500. Each denomination includes a portrait of a prominent Ukrainian on the front and a building or landmark on the back, and each has a different color scheme. For example, the 1-hryvnia bill is yellow-blue in color and bears a picture of Prince Vladimir I of the Kyivan Rus. The reverse side shows a wall of Vladimir's fortress.

Bartering was also widespread under Communism. People would trade goods they had and services they could provide rather than paying for them through official channels. People even found ways to barter for services such as home repairs and dental care.

By the time Ukraine became independent, the shadow economy and the barter system were fully established. It is impossible to measure the amount of money that changes hands in the shadow economy, so no one has accurate figures.

Bribery and the shadow economy go hand in hand. Police, judges, and other public officials are notorious for demanding and accepting bribes. Most Ukrainian business owners pay bribes when they need to obtain an operating license or a health permit. Since minor officials are poorly paid, they count on bribe money to enhance their incomes. "It's so complicated and so oppressive," lamented Lina Ratushny, a Kyiv business consultant. "The system is structured so that everyone here is guilty of corruption, because you are forced into it."

Because of Ukraine's shaky government and widespread corruption, foreign companies have been reluctant to invest in the country. However, Ukraine has recently introduced an anticorruption program, and the country has the potential to become a powerhouse in agriculture, manufacturing, and mining.

The Motor Sich company, based in Zaporizhzhya in southeastern Ukraine, is one of the world's largest manufacturers of airplane engines.

Products and Services

A nation's gross domestic product (GDP) is the total value of all of the goods and services it produces in a year. About 40 percent of Ukraine's GDP comes from the goods it produces. These include farm products, manufactured goods, and natural resources such as oil, minerals, and timber.

The remaining 60 percent of Ukraine's GDP comes from service industries. People who work in service industries provide services to others rather than producing goods that can be bought and sold. Doctors, teachers, salesclerks, police officers, and bankers all work in service industries.

Workers transport bins full of watermelons that have been unloaded from a barge in Kyiv.

From the Farms

In 2010, agriculture accounted for about 10 percent of Ukraine's GDP. With its fertile black soil, Ukraine is a leading producer of grain. Its farmers raise wheat, barley, corn, and rye. Other crops that are grown in abundance on Ukrainian farms include tobacco, sugar beets, potatoes, and sunflowers.

Farmers in Ukraine also raise livestock. Beef and dairy cattle graze on the grasses of the steppe. Pigs are raised all across the country, while sheep and goats are common in the Carpathian Mountains. Ukrainians also raise more than 180 million chickens, for both meat and eggs.

From the Factories

Ever since the Soviet era, Ukraine's eastern cities have been centers of industry. Ukraine's factories produce steel, machinery, chemical products, and vehicles such as cars, trucks, locomotives, railway freight cars, and ships. Many processed foods are manufactured in Ukraine, including sugar, vegetable oil, dairy products, and vegetables. Clothing, TVs, and appliances are also produced in the country.

Unfortunately, many of the nation's factories have been forced to use outdated equipment, a legacy of the

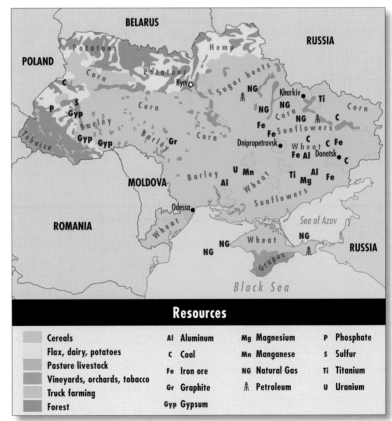

Resources

Cereals	**Al** Aluminum	**Mg** Magnesium	**P** Phosphate
Flax, dairy, potatoes	**C** Coal	**Mn** Manganese	**S** Sulfur
Pasture livestock	**Fe** Iron ore	**NG** Natural Gas	**Ti** Titanium
Vineyards, orchards, tobacco	**Gr** Graphite	Petroleum	**U** Uranium
Truck farming	**Gyp** Gypsum		
Forest			

What Ukraine Grows, Makes, and Mines

AGRICULTURE (2012)

Potatoes	23,250,200 metric tons
Sugar beets	18,438,900 metric tons
Wheat	15,762,600 metric tons

MANUFACTURING (VALUE IN SALES, 2012)

Food products	US$30,540,000,000
Metals	US$26,860,000,000
Textiles	US$11,860,000,000

MINING

Iron (2012)	73,934,000 metric tons
Coal (2012)	62,900,000 metric tons
Gypsum (2011)	676,000 metric tons

Soviet era. With the help of foreign investors, Ukrainian business owners hope to make their operations more efficient.

Fueling the Nation

Beneath Ukraine's soil lie vast deposits of coal. Ukraine is one of the world's top coal-producing countries. Ukraine burns 70 million metric tons of coal a year, and produces most of what it needs for its own use.

The situation is very different, however, when it comes to oil and natural gas. Ukraine imports about 75 percent of its gas and oil from Russia. Ukrainians depend on imported fuel to heat their homes and run their cars and buses. Any time

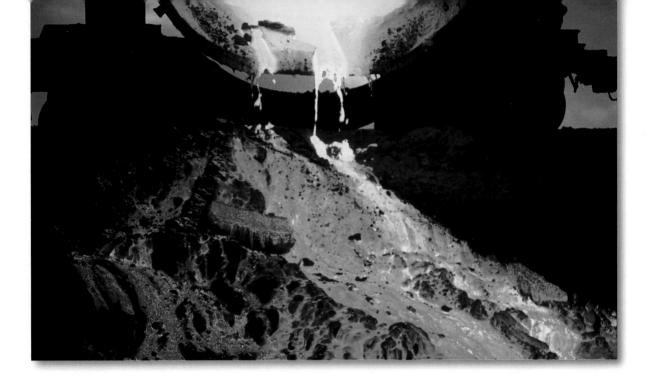

Russia raises its fuel prices, Ukrainians suffer.

Ukraine also has large deposits of iron ore, about one-fifth of all the iron in the world. Most of it is located in the central part of the country, in a region called the Kryvyy Rih Ore Basin. Ukraine also mines manganese, titanium, and mercury.

Workers dump the by-products of processing iron ore at a plant in Ukraine.

The Billionaire of Donetsk

Rynat Akhmetov (1966–) was born into a working-class Tatar family in Donetsk. Today, he is one of the richest people on earth, worth an estimated US$11.6 billion in 2014. Akhmetov runs System Capital Management (SCM), a vast corporation involved in everything from banking and real estate to mining, media, and telecommunications. With his unimaginable wealth, Akhmetov has acquired considerable power in governmental affairs.

CHAPTER 7

Who Are the Ukrainians?

A STRANGER VISITING A VILLAGE IN THE Carpathian Mountains once asked an old man to tell his life story. "I was born in Austro-Hungary, and I went to school in Czechoslovakia," the old man explained. "I served in the Hungarian army, and then I went to prison in the Soviet Union. Now I live in independent Ukraine."

The stranger was impressed. "You've certainly done a lot of traveling!" he exclaimed.

"Oh, no," the old man replied. "I've never left my village!"

Throughout their history, Ukrainians have endured a dizzying number of invasions and political upheavals. Yet somehow, through all the turmoil, they manage to hold on to a sense of themselves as a distinct people.

Opposite: **Young people walk through the streets of Lviv. Just one in four Ukrainians is under age twenty-five.**

The Crimean Tatars, A Displaced People

For nearly four centuries, beginning in the 1400s, the Crimean Tatars spread terror. Their armies swept into towns and villages to carry off women, children, and men, who were sold as slaves. Historians estimate that about two million people were sold into slavery during this grim period. In the twentieth century, however, the Crimean Tatars themselves endured terrible persecution. Between 1917 and 1933, more than half of the Crimean Tatars were deported or died. Then, in 1944, the Soviets drove all of the remaining Tatars from their Crimean homeland. They were sent to labor camps in Siberia and other faraway parts of Russia, where many of them died. In the 1980s, the surviving Crimean Tatars were allowed to return. Today, about 250,000 Crimean Tatars live in Crimea.

The Ethnic Puzzle

According to the 2013 census, Ukraine is home to 44,291,413 people. About 78 percent of these people are ethnically Ukrainian, and about 17 percent are of Russian descent.

Russian is the most widely spoken minority language in Ukraine. In general, Ukraine's Russian speakers live in Crimea and the eastern oblasts. Most people who speak Ukrainian can understand Russian fairly well. However, Russian speakers do not always speak or understand Ukrainian. Many people in Ukraine speak a mixture of the two languages, known as Surzhyk.

In addition to Ukrainians and Russians, Ukraine is home to many smaller ethnic groups. These include Romanians, Belarusians, Bulgarians, Hungarians, Poles, Jews, and Greeks.

The Carpathian region near the Polish border is home to several small Slavic groups, each with its own traditions and dialect, or form of the language. Among them are the Boykos, the Hutsuls, and the Rusyns.

People in Odessa attend a demonstration in support of Russian becoming an official language in Ukraine.

People of the Mountains

About twenty-one thousand Ukrainians refer to themselves as Hutsuls. The Hutsuls live in the mountains of western Ukraine and along the northern border of Romania. They speak a unique and ancient dialect of Ukrainian. Traditionally, the Hutsuls lived by cutting timber in the forests and herding sheep and cattle. A small, fleet-footed horse called the Hucul pony was first bred in Ukraine's Hutsul villages. Because the Hutsul population is so small, the Hutsul dialect and traditions are in danger of disappearing.

A woman in western Canada demonstrates Ukrainian folk dancing.

The Ukrainian Diaspora

A diaspora is the dispersion of a people from their homeland. Over the years, millions of people have been forced to leave Ukraine as a result of wars and economic hardship. This diaspora has created large Ukrainian communities throughout Europe and the Americas.

The largest Ukrainian populations outside Ukraine itself live in Russia and Canada. Nearly 2 million Ukrainians live in Russia, and Canada is home to about 1.2 million people of Ukrainian descent. Another 1 million live in the United States. Other countries with large Ukrainian populations are Romania, Bulgaria, Kazakhstan, Portugal, Brazil, and Argentina.

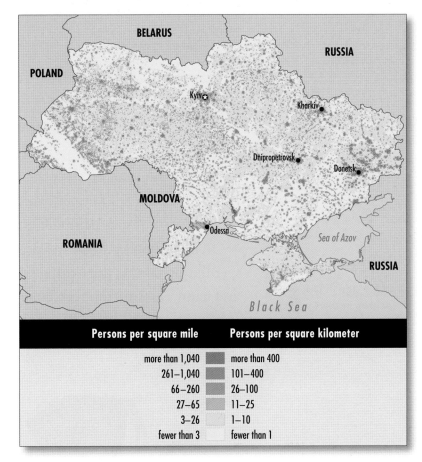

Most Ukrainians who have emigrated to other countries try to keep their language and traditions alive. Many attend Ukrainian church services, open Ukrainian businesses, and celebrate Ukrainian holidays.

About five million Ukrainians are currently working outside their native country. In general, Ukrainians who work abroad maintain close ties to their families back home. In 2012, they sent as much as US$7.5 billion to help support relatives and friends in Ukraine.

The Ukrainian Language

A linguist is a scholar who studies the origins and makeup of languages. Most linguists believe that the Ukrainian language arose sometime in the tenth century. It probably evolved from Old East Slavic, a language spoken in Kyivan Rus. The earli-

Population of Major Cities (2011 est.)	
Kyiv	2,829,000
Kharkiv	1,451,000
Odessa	1,010,000
Dnipropetrovsk	994,000
Donetsk	959,000

est known example of writing in Old East Slavic is a version of the Bible that was translated by Greek missionaries.

Like most languages, Ukrainian is constantly changing. Over the years it absorbed many words from Polish and Russian. Some Ukrainian words have German or Yiddish roots, and some can be traced to Greek, Turkish, and Latin.

In its written form, Ukrainian uses the Cyrillic alphabet. The Cyrillic alphabet is the writing system used in Russia, Mongolia, and many eastern European countries. The Ukrainian language uses thirty-two letters. When necessary, Ukrainian can also

A street sign in Odessa is written in the Cyrillic alphabet.

Now You're Speaking Ukrainian!

Here are a few basic Ukrainian words and phrases, transliterated into the Roman alphabet.

dobry dehn	hello
do pobacennja	good-bye
bud laska	please
dyakuyu	thank you
nema za sho	you're welcome
Yak vas zvaty?	What is your name?
Mene zvaty . . .	My name is . . .
tak	yes
nee	no

be written with the Roman alphabet that is used in western Europe and North America. Writing words of one language in the alphabet of another is called transliteration.

What's in a Name?

Names in Ukraine generally have three parts: the first name or given name, the middle name or patronymic, and the last name or surname. A person's middle name is based upon his or her father's given name. If the person is a male, his middle name is his father's first name followed by -vych or -ovych. If the person is a female, her middle name is her father's first name followed by –evna, -ovna, or -yvna. Thus, a boy whose father's given name is Aleksandr might be named Viktor Aleksandrovych Mereshenko. If a girl has a father named Pavlo, her name could be Natalya Pavlivna Ryterski. All three names are used in formal situations such as graduation ceremonies.

CHAPTER 8

The Rise of the Faithful

DURING THE DECADES UNDER SOVIET RULE, MOST Ukrainians drifted away from the practice of religion. Soviet authorities discouraged churchgoing and religious beliefs. Some religious ceremonies, such as church weddings, were strictly forbidden. Many churches were torn down. Others stopped holding services and were turned into museums. After Ukraine became independent in 1991, churches blossomed into life once more. Congregations swelled, new churches were built, Sunday schools opened, and people joyfully celebrated the holidays of the religious calendar. Among the freedoms the Ukrainian people had gained was the freedom to practice their faith.

Opposite: **Ukrainians light candles at a church in Kyiv.**

Pagan Roots

When Kyivan Rus emerged in the 800s CE, its people followed a polytheistic religion. Followers of a polytheistic religion worship many gods and goddesses who represent various aspects of nature and everyday life. When Prince Vladimir I took the throne in 980, he set up statues of the chief gods in front of his palace. There was a statue of Perun, the mighty god of thunder, with a head of silver and a mustache of gold. Veles was the god of prosperity. Dazhboh was the god of the sun, and Stryboh was the god of wind and water. Mokosh was the goddess of fertility and birth.

A statue of Perun in Dubno, in western Ukraine. Perun, usually depicted as a powerful man with a beard, was considered the keeper of order.

To win the favor of the gods and to stay in good standing with their ruler, the people of Kyivan Rus brought sacrifices every year to Prince Vladimir's palace. They laid baskets of their best fruits and vegetables before the statues, and they sacrificed their finest sheep, goats, and cattle. Sometimes they even brought sons and daughters, who were sacrificed as well.

Eight years after he took the throne, Prince Vladimir converted to Christianity. He chose the church of the Byzantine Empire to the south, the ancestor of today's Eastern Orthodox Church. Vladimir's conversion was a dramatic turning point in the history of Ukraine. The monarch ordered the statue of Perun to be dragged to the river and beaten with sticks. Then he commanded all of his subjects to gather on the banks of the Dnieper for baptism. According to an early historian, "Some stood up to their necks, others to their breasts, and the younger nearer the bank, some of them holding children in their arms."

The people of Kyivan Rus did not abandon their old gods after the mass baptism at the Dnieper. Instead, they gradually incorporated their old beliefs into the teachings of the Orthodox

Vladimir the Great helped bring Christianity to Ukraine.

The Cruel Saint

Vladimir I was not the first Ukrainian ruler to adopt Christianity. His grandmother, Princess Olga (890?–969), converted to the Byzantine faith in about 955. After her husband, Prince Igor, died, Princess Olga ruled Kyivan Rus from 945 to 957. In her effort to preserve the throne for her young son, she was merciless toward her enemies. By becoming a Christian, she strengthened her alliance with the Byzantine Empire. In spite of her legendary cruelty, Princess Olga was canonized, or made a saint, by the Orthodox Church in the thirteenth century.

Some Ukrainians bathe in icy waters on the Christian holiday of Epiphany to symbolically wash away their sins.

Church. For nearly a thousand years the church tried to stifle the ancient beliefs, which it referred to as paganism. Well into the twentieth century, Ukrainian villagers chanted spells to

The Ivana Kupala Festival

The Ivana Kupala Festival is a celebration of midsummer that dates to the pre-Christian era. It is celebrated on July 7. Kupala was the god of fertility and the harvest. The church tried to stamp out paganism by making this festival a feast day for St. John the Baptist. Villagers once believed that the earth revealed its secrets every year on Kupala Eve. It was said that ferns sprang up in places where treasure lay buried. Trees were said to speak aloud while witches gathered to dance. Herbs collected on Kupala Eve were believed to have the power to cure illnesses. Today, young couples search the woods for ferns, which are supposed to promise good luck and happiness. Some people bathe in streams and leap over roaring fires. Water and fire are believed to have cleansing properties.

bring rain, to ensure a good harvest, or to call down illness and disaster upon their enemies. Even today, some Christian holidays contain traces of old pagan celebrations.

One Land, Many Faiths

About 99 percent of Ukrainians consider themselves Christians. Of these, half belong to one of the several denominations of the Eastern Orthodox Church. The others are Roman Catholics (known as Polish Catholics in Ukraine), Ukrainian Greek Catholics, and Protestants. Ukraine also has small Muslim and Jewish populations.

The two largest churches are the Ukrainian Orthodox Church of the Moscow Patriarchate and the Ukrainian Orthodox Church of the Kyiv Patriarchate. The presiding

The Cathedral of St. George

Completed in 1760, the Cathedral of St. George served as the center of the Ukrainian Greek Catholic Church until 2005. It stands on a hill overlooking the city of Lviv. The most cherished object in the church is a seventeenth-century painting of Jesus's mother, Mary, which some people say has worked miracles. The cathedral is part of a complex that includes a belfry, a palace, and a garden.

Metropolitan Onufrius (with flowers) became the leader of the Ukrainian Orthodox Church of the Moscow Patriarchate in 2014.

leader, or metropolitan, of the Ukrainian Orthodox Church of the Moscow Patriarchate in Ukraine is appointed by church officials in Moscow. Church services are conducted in

Old Slavonic, a language that dates back to the Kyivan Rus. The Ukrainian Orthodox Church of the Kyiv Patriarchate was established in 1992 as Ukraine forged its own identity after independence. It uses both Ukrainian and Slavonic in services. The Ukrainian Autocephalous Orthodox Church is smaller. It conducts its services in Ukrainian.

When a man or boy enters an Orthodox church, he is expected to remove his hat. Women and girls, on the other hand, must cover their heads with a scarf or shawl. Orthodox churches do not have pews or chairs. It is considered sinful to sit during a church service. Throughout the service, which may last from two to seven hours, the congregation remains standing. Churchgoers are not required to stay for the entire service, however. It is quite acceptable to slip out early.

Worshippers fill a cathedral of the Ukrainian Orthodox Church of the Kyiv Patriarchate during a service celebrating the coming of Christianity to Kyivan Rus.

Holy Days

The Ukrainian Orthodox churches follow the Julian calendar, which was first adopted by the Roman emperor Julius Caesar in 45 BCE. In most countries, the Julian calendar was replaced by the Gregorian calendar in 1582. At the beginning of the twenty-first century, the Julian calendar was about thirteen days behind the Gregorian calendar. Thus, Christmas in Ukraine is celebrated on January 7 rather than December 25, when it is celebrated in the United States and Canada.

On Christmas Eve in Ukraine, carolers move from house to house, singing and carrying large open sacks. When carol-

Carolers sing following a Christmas service in central Ukraine.

Ukraine has a long tradition of making intricately decorated Easter eggs. The eggs, a symbol of life, are given to family members during the holiday.

ers stand below the window of a house, the homeowner drops candy, fruit, and other treats into their sacks. Ukrainian families feast upon special Christmas foods, including a braided bread called *kolach* and a blend of cooked wheat, honey, and poppy seeds called *kutya*.

Easter, the time when Jesus Christ is said to have risen from the dead, is the most important religious holiday of the year. The Easter season begins with Lent, a somber period of forty days when people avoid eating meat or dairy products. The

Religion in Ukraine

Ukrainian Orthodox (Moscow and Kyiv Patriarchates combined)	80%
Ukrainian Greek Catholic	8%
Ukrainian Autocephalous Orthodox	7%
Roman Catholic	2%
Protestant	2%
Other (including Jewish and Muslim)	1%

Ukrainians bring baskets of eggs, bread, cakes, and other goods to be blessed at Easter Mass.

Thursday before Easter is called Clean Thursday. Everything in the home is scrubbed to a shine in preparation for Easter.

On the evening of Holy Saturday, the day before Easter Sunday, people attend church services. The services begin at 11:30 p.m. and usually last until four in the morning. On Easter Sunday people exchange baskets filled with fluffy, braided bread called *paska* and beautifully decorated eggs called *pysanky*.

A Call for Unity

During the Maidan protests early in 2014, viewers around the world were horrified by footage of demonstrators mowed

The Orthodox Calendar	
Orthodox Christmas	January 7
Feast of Epiphany	January 19
Easter Sunday	March or April
Trinity Sunday	May or June

down by gunfire. At the same time, they were inspired by the bravery of the women and men who dared to take a stand for freedom. Among the heroes of those days were many Catholic and Orthodox priests. They buried the dead and prayed with the living. They even used their own bodies to protect the protesters from soldiers and snipers.

As the leaders and members of different churches worked and prayed side by side, their religious differences melted away. Some religious leaders began to talk about unifying the Ukrainian Orthodox churches. Cyril Hovorun, a former leader in the Ukrainian Orthodox Church of the Moscow Patriarchate,

Priests pray between police and protesters during the unrest in 2014.

explained, "Maidan, apart from being an important civil event, appeared to be an important religious event. There were prayers said every day in the morning and at night. . . . Maidan actually facilitated many churches, many church leaders who had never really conversed publicly with each other."

A leader of the Ukrainian Orthodox Church of the Kyiv Patriarchate wrote, "It is absolutely necessary for us to begin a dialogue leading to unification in a single local church of Kyiv. . . . We must pass from words about the necessity of being reunited to actions."

Each year, tens of thousands of Orthodox Jews from around the world come to Uman, in central Ukraine, on the Jewish new year to pray at the grave of Rabbi Nachman, a prominent Jewish leader.

Leaders of the Moscow Patriarchate approve of the idea of a united Ukrainian Orthodox Church—as long as it is united under Moscow. Whether Moscow or Kyiv will prevail remains an open question.

Jews and Muslims

At its peak in the early twentieth century, the Jewish population of Ukraine was probably about 2.7 million. Many of these Jews were starved like their fellow Ukrainians, others were killed in pogroms, and still more were murdered in World War II. Many others moved to other parts of the world. By 2014, Ukraine's Jewish population was estimated to be between two hundred thousand and four hundred thousand. The largest community is in Kyiv. Other cities such as Dnipropetrovsk, Kharkiv, and Odessa also have large Jewish populations.

Most Muslims in Ukraine today are Crimean Tatars. While Crimea has the largest proportion of Muslims in Ukraine, Muslims live in all major cities in the country.

Muslim Tatars exchange greetings after a service at a mosque in Kharkiv.

CHAPTER 9

A Strong Spirit

UKRAINE HAS SUFFERED THROUGH WAR AND FAMINE. Its language and culture have been suppressed. Nevertheless, the Ukrainian spirit remains unbroken. Ukrainians express themselves in art, literature, music, and dance.

Early Ukrainian Literature

Ukrainian literature dates back to Kyivan Rus. Literature from this age was written in the Old East Slavic and Old Church Slavonic languages. These writings include sermons, proverbs, and translations of sections of the Bible.

Other writings from Kyivan Rus include the early chronicles. Blending history and legend, the chronicles trace the story of Kyivan Rus from its beginnings until 1292. Historians believe that the chronicles had several original authors, and that they were copied by scribes again and again through the centuries. The most famous epic poem of Kyivan Rus is *The Tale of Igor's Campaign*, which was written in about 1187. This long poem recounts the story of a doomed military expedition led by a prince of Kyivan Rus. The manuscript was discovered in the eighteenth century but was later destroyed in a fire.

After the Tatars conquered Kyivan Rus in 1240, Ukrainian literature almost disappeared. It began to revive the following century and blossomed further when the first printing press in what is now Ukraine began operating in Lviv in 1574. Much of what was printed had to do with religion. There were sermons and lives of the saints. But many works arguing about religion, the church, and politics were also printed. These materials could be printed quickly and distributed easily. Soon, presses in several other cities were

The Ostroh Bible was the first complete Bible written in Old Church Slavonic. It was printed in 1581 in Ostroh, in western Ukraine.

A statue of Hryhorii Skovoroda stands in a park in Kyiv.

also churning out printed pages. As printed material became more available, more and more people learned to read.

Most of this printed material was written in Polish or in Old Church Slavonic. The language of Ukraine's towns and villages was spoken by farmers and shopkeepers, but it did not yet have a written form.

Telling the Story

One influential writer in Ukraine was Hryhorii Skovoroda (1722–1794). After a brief teaching career, Skovoroda spent his life wandering the roads of eastern Ukraine, thinking and writing. Some of his songs, fables, and poems have become woven into Ukraine's folklore.

By the end of the eighteenth century, eastern Ukraine was under the influence of Russia. Russian was the language for poems and scholarly works. But literary Ukrainian began to

The Shape of the Poem

The names of most Ukrainian poets of the sixteenth and seventeenth centuries have been lost to history. However, many poems by unknown authors have survived. A number of these poems were written as acrostics. An acrostic is a poem in which the first letter of each line can be read from top to bottom down the page to spell a word or name.

In another type of poem, the lines on the page form the shape of a cross, a half-moon, or a pyramid. The most unusual poems of this period are called crabs. A crab is a poem that can be read either from left to right or right to left.

emerge. Ivan Kotlyarevsky (1769–1838) is usually regarded as the father of Ukrainian vernacular literature, or literature written in the language of the people. His great epic poem *Eneida* was a humorous retelling of the great Roman epic *Aeneid*.

More Ukrainians began turning away from Russian to write in their own language about their history and way of life. Several collections of folk songs were published. Scholars started to rec-

Ivan Kotlyarevsky was honored on a Soviet stamp in 1969. He wrote several plays that became classics in Ukraine.

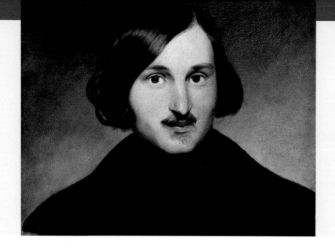

Writing in Russian

Some of Ukraine's finest authors chose to write in Russian. The novelist and playwright Nikolai Gogol wrote in the Russian language. He is remembered for such work as his comedy *The Inspector General*, a play that pokes fun at Russian bureaucracy and small-town corruption.

ognize that the Ukrainian language was richly expressive. They realized that it could be a vehicle for serious thought. Russian authorities were alarmed by this surge of interest in Ukrainian culture. They forbade schools to teach reading and writing in Ukrainian. Respect for the Ukrainian language became a core part of Ukraine's budding patriotic movement.

No writer embodied Ukraine's patriotic ideals more fully than Taras Shevchenko (1814–1861), Ukraine's most-beloved poet. Shevchenko's first collection of poetry, *Kobzar*, appeared in 1840. His epic poem, *Haidamaky*, was published in the following year. In 1847, Shevchenko was imprisoned and then exiled for belonging to a secret society that supported equal rights for all and the development of national cultures in the region. Although he was eventually released, he never managed to return to Ukraine.

Shevchenko's life and work had a profound influence on Panas Myrny (1849–1920). Myrny's best-known work is a novel called *Propashcha Syla* (*The Ruined Strength*). It is sometimes known by the title *Khiba Revut Voly, Iak Iasla Povni?* that translates as *Do the Oxen Bellow When Their Mangers Are Full?* The novel covers a century in the life of a Ukrainian village under the yoke of serfdom.

Lesia Ukrainka wrote poetry, plays, and political and literary essays.

Ukraine's first notable woman writer was Mariia Vilinska (1834–1907), who wrote under the pen name Marko Vovchok. Although she was born in Russia, she moved to Ukraine and became fascinated by its language and culture. Her collection of short stories, *Folk Stories*, was published in 1857. Like Panas Myrny, she wrote about the injustices of serfdom. Her stories also expose the plight of women, who had few rights during her lifetime.

In the 1860s and 1870s Russia passed laws that forbade the publication of writings in Ukrainian. Galicia became the heart of Ukrainian literature because it was not under Russian control. Ivan Franko was the most prominent writer in Galicia during this period. A highly versatile writer, he was at home with poetry, fiction, drama, and literary criticism.

Like many Ukrainian writers of the twentieth century, the poet Lesia Ukrainka (1871–1913) was a dedicated political activist who opposed tsarist Russia. A monument to Lesia Ukrainka stands in Kyiv on a street that is named in her memory.

After the tsar was overthrown during the Russian Revolution of 1917, Ukrainian writers had a brief period of freedom and creativity. Tragically, this era crashed to a halt in

the 1930s, when Joseph Stalin rose to power. Stalin required writers to churn out works that praised the Communist Party. Hundreds of writers were murdered, sent to work camps, or driven to suicide when they refused to cooperate.

Even after the death of Stalin in 1953, Ukrainian writers were forced to follow strict Communist Party lines. Freedom of expression did not return to Ukraine until the final years of the USSR. The works of many writers found their way back into print, and new voices began to emerge. Novelists such as Valerii Shevchuk published vital works in the 1980s. Ukrainian independence opened the way for an eager generation of young poets, novelists, and playwrights brimming with ideas and ready to create a fresh new literature for their homeland.

Valerii Shevchuk writes stories that delve deeply into the minds of ordinary people.

The Art of the Fresco

Fresco is an art form that involves painting on a plaster surface. Powdered paints are applied to the plaster while it is still wet. This means that the mural becomes part of the wall, rather than being painted onto the wall. Frescoes are very durable, and the technique can be used to decorate both the interiors of buildings and the outsides.

Plaster, Paint, and Stone

Warfare destroyed much of Ukraine's early artwork, but some splendid examples managed to survive. Archaeologists have discovered frescoes dating back to the fourth century BCE. These pictures adorned the homes and tombs of Greek colonists who settled along the Black Sea. In Kyivan Rus, frescoes in the churches depicted biblical scenes and the lives of the saints. Magnificent frescoes have been preserved at the Saint Sophia Cathedral and the church of St. Cyril's Monastery in Kyiv.

Mosaic is another ancient art form that has a long history in Ukraine. Mosaics are made by embedding small pieces of colored tile, glass, ceramic, or stone in wet plaster or cement. Mosaics decorated the floor of a bath built in the Greek colony of Chersonese Taurica during the third century BCE. Like frescoes, mosaics were used to decorate churches during the Kyivan Rus period. Fine mosaics can be seen at the Saint Sophia Cathedral and the Dormition Cathedral of the Kyivan Cave Monastery. Both the fresco and mosaic art forms originated in ancient Greece and were developed further in the Byzantine Empire. The artists who decorated the churches and cathedrals in Kyivan Rus were brought from Constantinople, the capital of the Byzantine Empire, to do this highly skilled work.

Icon painting, too, had its roots in the Byzantine Empire, but Ukrainians quickly made it their own. Icons are images of holy people painted in a stylized manner. Some students learned the art of icon painting at the Kyivan Cave Monastery as early as the 1100s. By the early 1400s, several more schools had sprung up in Galicia and other parts of western Ukraine to train icon painters. Icon painting flourished well into the eighteenth century. Icons decorate churches throughout Ukraine, and small icons are often seen in homes as well.

During the Kyivan Rus period, the church frowned upon the creation of three-dimensional figures. Today, most religious sculpture in Ukraine is found in Greek and Roman Catholic churches near the Polish border.

One of Ukraine's most innovative sculptors, Alexander Archipenko (1887–1964), left the country shortly before the Russian Revolution.

Mosaics at Saint Sophia Cathedral date to the eleventh century. These mosaics influenced the art in churches throughout Ukraine.

A Strong Spirit   **111**

What Is an Icon?

An icon is an image of a holy person painted in a style common in Orthodox churches. The image is usually painted on wood, but icons can also be murals, mosaics, tapestries, or sculptures. The images usually have strong outlines and deep colors. They are sometimes decorated with gold leaf, extremely thin sheets of gold. Some Orthodox churches feature an iconostasis, a large screen filled with icons. The many icons on the screen are separated by columns.

Working in Paris, France, he gained a strong international reputation. Archipenko produced profoundly modern work, mixing abstraction and human forms.

Like Ukraine's writers, artists were persecuted during the 1930s under the regime of Joseph Stalin. In the years after World War II, artists were required to support the goals of the Soviet system. They painted murals showing smiling factory workers as they assembled trucks and tractors, and designed posters depicting Lenin, Stalin, and other Soviet leaders. A scattering of Ukrainian artists continued to create their own work, but they were not allowed to show it in public exhibitions.

Ivan Rutkovych, Master of the Iconostasis

Born sometime around 1650, Ivan Rutkovych was among the finest of Ukraine's icon painters. His iconostasis from the Church of Christ's Nativity in Zhovkva now stands in the Lviv National Museum. His work also can be seen in the iconostasis of Holy Trinity Church in Zhovkva.

Independent Ukraine provides a welcoming climate for painters and sculptors. At last, after decades of suppression, the arts are free to thrive once more.

The Joy of Song

Music is deeply rooted in Ukrainian culture. Much of Ukraine's early music was composed for religious services. Certain songs were sung to celebrate spring planting, and others were sung at funerals.

Among Ukraine's traditional instruments are the *bandura*, sometimes called the *kobza*. It is a large, pear-shaped instrument that can have as many as sixty-eight strings. The *relya* is a type of hurdy-gurdy, a string instrument that is played by turning a crank that rubs a wheel against the strings. Ukrainian folk music also uses a three-stringed cello called the *basolya* and bagpipes called *volynka*.

"The Carol of the Bells"

One of the most popular Christmas songs sung in North America is "The Carol of the Bells." The song was written in 1918 by the Ukrainian composer Mykola Leontovych. It is based on an ancient chant known as "Shchedryk," which was sung in honor of spring. The original lyrics describe a swallow flying to a house and bringing good luck. Western audiences first heard the song in 1921 when it was performed at New York's Carnegie Hall by the Ukrainian National Chorus. Today, it is performed by choirs around the world during the Christmas season.

Folk dancing is an exciting art form in Ukraine. Dancers jump, twirl, clap, and shout to rollicking tunes played by a band with a fiddle, flute, and drum. A dance called the *hopak* dates back to the Cossacks. While the women sway and circle, the men show their skill with leaps, turns, and lightning-fast kicks.

Ukrainians perform an energetic dance.

Singers on the Road

For centuries, musicians called *kobzari* traveled from village to village in Ukraine, singing for coins or meals. The kobzari were highly trained and belonged to a special guild of musicians. Most of the kobzari were blind. Their ballads told of peasant rebellions, Cossack uprisings, and other attacks on authority. In 1933, some three hundred kobzari were invited to attend a conference on folk music in the city of Kharkiv. The invitation was a cruel trick. When the musicians arrived for the conference, Stalin's police were waiting. The police rounded the kobzari up, and they were all executed. Today, a kobzari is portrayed on Ukraine's 100-hryvnia bill.

During the 1960s, Soviet leaders encouraged a revival of Ukrainian folk music and dance. Folk choirs sang formal, staged versions of songs that had been handed down for generations in the villages.

Nina Matviyenko is an outstanding performer of Ukrainian folk songs and modern music. She has sung in Ukrainian films and has performed for audiences from France to Mexico. Matviyenko has been honored as the People's Artist of Ukraine.

Sports and Games

Ukrainians love sports and outdoor activities. After school, children take part in tennis, soccer, and other team sports. Like most Europeans, Ukrainians are wild about soccer. The country's most popular team is the Dynamo Kyiv, which plays in Kyiv's Lobanovsky Dynamo Stadium. Dynamo Kyiv belongs to the Ukrainian Premier League. Basketball, ice hockey,

Soccer is the most popular sport in Ukraine.

rugby, volleyball, and cricket are all popular team sports in Ukraine. Individual sports popular in Ukraine include boxing, wrestling, swimming, and track and field.

For years the USSR excelled in the Olympic Games. The Soviets considered Olympic success a triumph of the Communist system over the non-Communist world. Soviet

Olympic Protest

The 2014 Winter Olympics were held in Sochi, Russia. Skiers from Ukraine won the gold medal in women's relay biathlon. But controversy followed the Ukrainian athletes even onto the ski slopes and ice-skating rinks. The Ukrainian team asked to wear black armbands to protest the violence raging in their country. The International Olympic Committee refused the team's request, arguing that the armbands would be disrespectful to the international nature of the games. As a result of this decision, some Ukrainian athletes refused to compete and returned home. Said skier Bogdana Matsotska, "I don't want to participate when in my country people are dying."

Champion Gymnast

Rhythmic gymnastics is a wildly popular sport in Ukraine. Teams of up to five members manipulate balls or clubs in intricate patterns. When performed properly, the sport is a delightful blend of ballet and gymnastics. Ukraine's Anna Bessonova (1984–) is a world-class athlete in this sport. Those who knew her as a child in Kyiv were not surprised by her success, considering her family background. Her father was a star football player on the Dynamo Kyiv team, and her mother was a world champion gymnast.

leaders poured money into training facilities and sports stadiums. Because of this emphasis on sports, Ukraine has a wealth of athletic fields, sports stadiums, and swimming pools. Ukraine and other former Soviet republics continue to benefit from the Soviet push for excellence in athletics.

At the 1996 Summer Games, Ukraine competed in the Olympics for the first time as an independent nation. Ukraine did well, earning a total of twenty-three medals, nine of them gold. The star of the 1996 games was Lilia Podkopayeva, who won gold medals for women's individual gymnastics and women's floor exercise.

On the weekends, people flock to the countryside to relax. With the Black Sea to the south, it is no surprise that swimming and boating are favorite sports in Ukraine. However, water sports are not confined to the seacoast. Kyiv has miles of public beaches that stretch along the banks of the Dnieper River. Lakes in the capital city also provide opportunities for swimming and rowing.

CHAPTER 10

A Warm Welcome

ONE OF THE MOST POPULAR UKRAINIAN FOLK-
tales is about a mouse and a mitten. One cold, windy day, a
mouse wandered through the forest in search of a place to live
for the winter. He was delighted when he discovered a woolen
mitten that someone had dropped in the snow. He crept into
the mitten and curled up for a warm nap.

Pretty soon a rabbit hopped along, shivering in the cold.
The mouse invited him in, and the rabbit crawled into the
mitten, too. Next a partridge came calling. Then a frog, a
squirrel, and even a wolf. The mouse welcomed each of them
into his home. Somehow the little mitten stretched and
stretched to make room for everyone.

The mouse's welcoming spirit symbolizes Ukrainian hospi-
tality. No matter how little they have, Ukrainians are ready to
share it with visitors.

Opposite: **Soldiers
distribute flowers to
women outside a military
base on Ukrainian
Mothers' Day.**

Elderly Ukrainians wait at a bus stop. On average, Ukrainians live to age sixty-nine.

At Home in Ukraine

Most Ukrainians who live in cities reside in small apartments. Many apartment buildings have a wide patio out front. If the weather is pleasant, children play on the patio while the adults sit and read or chat. Older women, known as babushkas, keep an eye on everything that goes on around them.

Although apartments are small, Ukrainians make room for family members. Often, a two-bedroom apartment is home to a mother and father, two children, and grandparents. An aunt and uncle may move in for a few months while they look for a place of their own. When a cousin arrives from the country to look for a job, someone finds her a spot where she can sleep on the floor.

Ukrainians are as generous with food as they are with living space. Visitors always get the best and the biggest portions. Women do nearly all of the cooking, and junk food is almost unknown. Every meal includes fresh fruits and vegetables. People shop at local markets or grow vegetables in their own gardens.

Automobiles are expensive in Ukraine. Bus fares are cheap, and the buses run everywhere. Most people take the bus to work and walk to and from the nearby shops.

Good to Eat

Food in Ukraine is delicious and filling. Bread is a staple food. In much of Ukraine, rye bread is common. In the south, people tend to eat wheat bread. In addition to everyday breads, Ukrainians eat special breads for holidays and celebrations. These include *babka* and *paska*, breads served on Easter, and a ring-shaped bread called *kolach*, which is often served on Christmas.

A woman sells bread at a shop in Lviv. Bread is an important part of most Ukrainian meals.

Dumplings are also popular in Ukraine. They are filled with everything from cheese to cabbage to fish to plums. Potatoes are common with meals. They are boiled, baked, put in dumplings, or made into potato pancakes. Many different vegetables are used in Ukrainian cooking, including cabbages, cucumbers, beets, and carrots.

Soups are served with many meals in Ukraine. The most popular soup is borscht. No two cooks make borscht in quite the same way, but it usually features beets, cabbage, and beef. It can be served cold on a hot summer day or piping hot in the winter. Borscht is so popular in Ukraine that it is considered the national soup.

Borscht is often served with a hearty, dark bread.

Potato Pancakes

Potato pancakes are a delicious side dish served with many meals in Ukraine. Have an adult help you with this recipe.

Ingredients

5 medium potatoes

1 onion

1 egg

3 tablespoons flour

1 tablespoon sour cream, plus 1 cup

1 teaspoon salt

Pepper to taste

Vegetable oil

Directions

Peel the potatoes and onions. Grate them into a large bowl, and mix thoroughly. Add the egg, flour, and 1 tablespoon of sour cream, and stir until it is mixed. Then add salt and pepper and stir. Pour 2 tablespoons of vegetable oil in a pan, and place it over medium-high heat on the stove. When the oil is hot, drop large dollops of the batter into the pan, making sure they are not touching. Fry the pancakes until they are golden brown. Then flip them over and fry the other sides. Remove the pancakes from the pan and drain the excess oil. Add more oil to the pan, and make more pancakes until the batter is gone. Serve the potato pancakes with sour cream. Enjoy!

Living in the Country

In many ways, the Ukrainian village has changed little in the past hundred years. People still carry buckets to the local well to fetch water for washing and bathing. Power outages happen frequently. Some places have Internet access, but the connection is sometimes unreliable.

In the twenty-first century, one invention transformed village life—the cell phone. Many villages never had telephone service until cell phones became common. Now teens text their friends, exchange YouTube videos, and share messages on Facebook. Families can talk to friends and relatives all over the globe. With the cell phone, rural Ukraine is connected to the wider world.

A navy cadet calls his parents before an Independence Day parade.

Wedding Day

During the Soviet era, most Ukrainian weddings were performed by a judge or city clerk. The bride and groom laid flowers before a war monument or a statue of Lenin. After Ukraine became independent, couples began to hold fancy church weddings, followed by elaborate receptions.

In current custom, before the wedding ceremony the bride embroiders a supply of white cloths called *rushnyky*, which are often given as gifts. After the wedding, the couple may lay flowers before a statue of the national poet, Taras Shevchenko. Wedding bouquets always have five, seven, nine, or some other odd number of flowers. Bouquets of even-numbered flowers are used only for funerals.

The wedding reception is a huge affair that may last up to three days. Friends and relatives continue to celebrate together, even after the bride and groom depart for their honeymoon. The toastmaster, or *tamada*, calls for songs, dancing, and endless toasts.

Going to School

About 99.7 percent of all Ukrainians are literate, meaning that they know how to read and write. Ukraine has one of the highest literacy rates in the world. All Ukrainian children are required to enter school by the age of six. A basic education involves eleven years of schooling. Elementary and middle school programs, from first through ninth grade, are usually housed in one building.

During middle school (fifth through ninth grades) students study a variety of subjects, including Ukrainian literature, a foreign language, algebra, geometry, biology, chemistry, and

Young children in Ukraine attend school from September through May.

physics. Classes in each subject meet once or twice a week. During the school day students also take part in activities such as chess, choir, and marching band.

During ninth and eleventh grades, students take a series of exams called the Independent Government Tests. These tests are somewhat like the college entrance exams used in the United States and Canada. Good test scores will ensure admission to a university and may help the student qualify for a scholarship.

Ukraine has major universities in Kyiv, Kharkiv, Odessa, Lviv, and other cities. The National Academy of Sciences of Ukraine is the nation's largest scientific institution. Its headquarters is in Kyiv.

Ukrainians love the outdoors. On weekends and holidays they head for the countryside with fishing poles, water skis,

or binoculars. A favorite destination is Mount Hoverla, the highest peak in the nation.

After Ukraine became independent in 1991, Mount Hoverla became the focus of a new tradition. Each year on Ukraine's Independence Day, August 24, Ukrainians hike up Mount Hoverla to take in the view from its summit. A panorama of mountains, streams, and villages stretches in all directions. As they gaze about them, their hair tossed by the wind, the people may reflect upon their nation's long and troubled history, and look forward to a promising future.

Big Bear's Den

Big Bear's Den is a game that Ukrainian children play in the snow. First, they use a stick to draw a large square on the surface of the snow. The square must be big enough for several children to stand inside. Then, inside the large square, they draw a smaller square. That square is the bear's den. One child, the bear, stands in the den, while the others wait in the outer square. The "bear" shouts, "The bear is coming!" and rushes to tag one of the other children. Holding hands, the two return to the bear's den, only to rush out again and tag someone else. All of the children who have been tagged must hold hands whenever they leave the bear's den. The last child to be tagged is the bear in the next round.

Timeline

UKRAINIAN HISTORY

The Trypillian culture arises in what is now Ukraine.	**ca. 4000 BCE**
Scythians gain control of the steppe; Greek colonies are established along the Black Sea.	**600s BCE**
Slavs begin migrating into what is now Ukraine.	**500s CE**
Varangians from Scandinavia become dominant in the region.	**800s**
The Kyivan Rus state is formed.	**mid-800s**
Vladimir I of Kyivan Rus requires his people to accept Christianity.	**988**
Construction begins on Saint Sophia Cathedral.	**1037**
Tatars from central Asia invade Kyivan Rus and destroy Kyiv.	**1240**
Most of what is now Ukraine becomes part of the Polish-Lithuanian Commonwealth.	**1569**
The first printing press in what is now Ukraine begins operation in Lviv.	**1574**
A Cossack named Bohdan Khmelnytsky leads a rebellion against the Polish rulers.	**1648**
Ukraine is partitioned between Poland and Russia.	**1667**

WORLD HISTORY

ca. 2500 BCE	The Egyptians build the pyramids and the Sphinx in Giza.
ca. 563 BCE	The Buddha is born in India.
313 CE	The Roman emperor Constantine legalizes Christianity.
610	The Prophet Muhammad begins preaching a new religion called Islam.
1054	The Eastern (Orthodox) and Western (Roman Catholic) Churches break apart.
1095	The Crusades begin.
1215	King John seals the Magna Carta.
1300s	The Renaissance begins in Italy.
1347	The plague sweeps through Europe.
1453	Ottoman Turks capture Constantinople, conquering the Byzantine Empire.
1492	Columbus arrives in North America.
1500s	Reformers break away from the Catholic Church, and Protestantism is born.

UKRAINIAN HISTORY

Russia gains control of most of Ukraine; Galicia becomes part of Austria's Habsburg Empire.	Late 1700s
Peasants are freed from serfdom.	1861
A revolution breaks out in Russia.	1917
Ukrainians announce the formation of an independent nation, the Ukrainian National Republic.	1918
Ukraine becomes part of the Union of Soviet Socialist Republics (USSR).	1922
Ukraine's farms begin to be collectivized.	1929
Soviet authorities send most of Ukraine's crops elsewhere, triggering a famine that kills at least four million people.	1932–1933
German troops invade Ukraine and other parts of the Soviet Union.	1941
The worst nuclear accident in world history occurs at the Chernobyl Nuclear Power Plant.	1986
The Soviet Union dissolves; Ukraine declares its independence.	1991
Ukraine adopts a constitution.	1996
In the Orange Revolution, mass demonstrations against election fraud lead to new presidential elections.	2004
The Maidan protest movement begins, with demonstrators demanding that Ukraine be more closely tied to the European Union.	2013
Crimea votes to secede from Ukraine; Russia annexes Crimea.	2014

WORLD HISTORY

1776	The U.S. Declaration of Independence is signed.
1789	The French Revolution begins.
1865	The American Civil War ends.
1879	The first practical lightbulb is invented.
1914	World War I begins.
1917	The Bolshevik Revolution brings communism to Russia.
1929	A worldwide economic depression begins.
1939	World War II begins.
1945	World War II ends.
1969	Humans land on the Moon.
1975	The Vietnam War ends.
1989	The Berlin Wall is torn down as communism crumbles in Eastern Europe.
1991	The Soviet Union breaks into separate states.
2001	Terrorists attack the World Trade Center in New York City and the Pentagon near Washington, D.C.
2004	A tsunami in the Indian Ocean destroys coastlines in Africa, India, and Southeast Asia.
2008	The United States elects its first African American president.

Fast Facts

Official name: Ukraine

Capital: Kyiv

Official language: Ukrainian

Kyiv

National flag

Black Sea coast

Official religion:	None
Type of government:	Republic
Head of state:	President
Head of government:	Prime minister
National anthem:	"The State Anthem of Ukraine"
Area of country:	233,090 square miles (603,700 sq km)
Latitude and longitude of geographic center:	49°N, 32°E
Bordering countries:	Russia to the east and northeast; Belarus to the northwest; Poland, Slovakia, and Hungary to the west; and Romania and Moldova to the southwest
Highest elevation:	Mount Hoverla, 6,762 feet (2,061 m) above sea level
Lowest elevation:	Sea level along the Black Sea
Average high temperature:	In Kyiv, 30°F (–1°C) in January, 78°F (26°C) in July
Average low temperature:	In Kyiv, 22°F (–6°C) in January, 61°F (16°C) in July
Average annual precipitation:	30 inches (76 cm) in the north; 9 inches (23 cm) in the south
Highest recorded temperature:	108°F (42°C) at Luhansk on August 12, 2010
Lowest recorded temperature:	–26°F (–32°C) in Kyiv, February 9, 1929

Lviv

National population (2013): 44,291,413

Population of major cities (2011 est.):

Kyiv	2,829,000
Kharkiv	1,451,000
Odessa	1,010,000
Dnipropetrovsk	994,000
Donetsk	959,000

Landmarks:
- ▶ *Carpathian Biosphere Reserve*, Rakhiv
- ▶ *Cathedral of St. George*, Lviv
- ▶ *Mariinsky Palace*, Kyiv
- ▶ *Potemkin Stairs*, Odessa
- ▶ *Saint Sophia Cathedral*, Kyiv

Economy: Ukraine's leading farm products include corn, wheat, barley, potatoes, and sunflowers. Farmers also raise cattle, pigs, and chickens. Major manufactured goods include iron, fertilizers, machinery, and railroad cars. Processed foods are also a major industry. Ukraine produces most of the coal it needs for domestic use. It also mines iron, manganese, titanium, and mercury.

Currency: The hryvnia. In 2014, 1 hryvnia equaled about US$0.08, and US$1.00 equaled about 13 hryvni.

Currency

System of weights and measures: Metric system

Literacy rate: 99.7%

Schoolchildren

Ivan Kotlyarevsky

Common Ukrainian words and phrases:

dobry dehn	hello
do pobacennja	good-bye
bud laska	please
dyakuyu	thank you
nema za sho	you're welcome
Yak vas zvaty?	What is your name?
Mene zvaty . . .	My name is . . .
tak	yes
nee	no

Prominent Ukrainians:

Rynat Akhmetov	(1966–)
Businessperson	
Anna Bessonova	(1984–)
Olympic gymnast	
Bohdan Khmelnytsky	(ca. 1595–1657)
Cossack leader	
Ivan Kotlyarevsky	(1769–1838)
Poet and philosopher	
Nina Matviyenko	(1947–)
Singer	
Taras Shevchenko	(1814–1861)
Poet	
Yulia Tymoshenko	(1960–)
Politician	
Vladimir I	(ca. 956–1015)
Leader of Kyivan Rus	

To Find Out More

Books

- ▶ Bassis, Vladimir. *Ukraine*. New York: Cavendish Square, 2007.

- ▶ Brett, Jan. *The Mitten: A Ukrainian Folktale*. New York: G. P. Putnam's Sons, 2009.

- ▶ Shevchenko, Anna. *Ukraine: The Essential Guide to Customs and Culture*. London: Kuperard, 2012.

Music

- ▶ Ukrainian Bandura Players. *Songs and Dances of Ukraine*. New York: Monitor Records, 2012.

- ▶ *Ukrainian Village Music*. El Cerrito, CA: Arhoolie Music, 2011.

▶ Visit this Scholastic Web site for more information on Ukraine:
www.factsfornow.scholastic.com
Enter the keyword **Ukraine**

Index

Page numbers in *italics*
indicate illustrations.

Meet the Author

DEBORAH KENT GREW UP IN LITTLE FALLS, NEW Jersey. In 1959, at the height of the Cold War, her parents spent three weeks traveling in the Soviet Union to gather some first-hand knowledge of life there. For years afterward, Kent heard stories of their amazing adventures in Kyiv, Odessa, and other Ukrainian cities, as well as the rest of the USSR.

Kent has been writing books for young readers since her first novel, *Belonging*, was published by Dial Press in 1978. She has written nearly two dozen young adult novels as well as more than one hundred titles on history and geography for middle grade readers. Her most recent titles for Scholastic are *Mexico*, in the Enchantment of the World Series, and *U.S. Infrastructure*.

In researching this book, Kent read extensively about Ukraine, its people, and its history. She would like to express special thanks to the staff of the Ukrainian National Museum of Chicago. Exploring the museum's wonderful collection of folk art, artifacts, agricultural tools, and musical instruments opened up Ukraine's history and culture.

Photo Credits